OBSTACLES . . .
BRING 'EM

Obstacles . . .
Bring 'Em

Maria Federici (Doyle)

Library of Congress Control Number: 2013913193
ISBN: Hardcover   978-1-4836-7360-8
               Softcover   978-1-4836-7359-2
               Ebook   978-1-4836-7361-5

Rev. date: 07/24/2013

To order additional copies of this book, contact:
Xlibris LLC
1-888-795-4274
www.Xlibris.com
Orders@Xlibris.com
135849

CONTENTS

Thank you to all involved, especially Mr. Joseph A. Dick.

INTRODUCTION

I was born in 1979. I could say, for instance, that I was born the same year that the United States and China began diplomatic relations or that it was the year of a record blizzard. But that's just historical current events and doesn't really tell you anything about me.

If you want to know anything about me from that year, I'd say that's the year that Pink Floyd premiered *The Wall*, that "YMCA" by the Village People hit number 2 on the charts, and the YMCA sued the Village People for libel. Meanwhile the Dukes of Hazzard premiered, bringing "Daisy Dukes" to the world of fashion, so to speak.

Those are all interesting and important things, but none of those things makes me important; the only thing that makes me important is that I am a human being.

I went to elementary school, junior high school, and high school. Most of us did. I went to college. A lot of us did. I like music. Most of us do. I like dogs. A lot of us do. I like accomplishing things—I do; how about you?

I enjoy the company of friends. Well, who the heck doesn't!

I had a tough life growing up. Didn't we all? And despite having it tough, I got through school, and I went to college; and like a lot of kids who went to college, I held more than a few jobs in order to pay my way.

Sure, we all work, and we all work hard. I worked hard at tending bar. Oh, it sounds like an easy job; just slop a few drinks around, and everybody pays you for just showing up, right? It has to be easy to become a popular bartender. It's just an inside track to become a VIP bartender at a top club in a major city, right?

Right.

Could you—would you—be willing to put up the effort required to get there?

I did.

It feels good to see someone come through the door just because you're working there. It feels even better when they call ahead—just to see if you're working.

I know you don't really need it explained to you, but you do understand that it meant they would have gone somewhere else, right? It wasn't the bar or the club or the restaurant; it was *you* that made them choose or not choose to come be a patron of where you work.

Patron is an interesting word. The dictionary defines *patron* as a person who gives financial support to a person, organization, cause, or activity; or more simply, a customer, especially a regular one, at a theater, a store, a restaurant.

And patrons can be easygoing or difficult people. Just ask any artist; patrons can be wonderful or hard to deal with.

Now you may think that patrons just support some sort of high-falutin', prose-writing, music-composing, paint-slinging things—a patron of the arts is what they say, right? And all those are just fine. I like the fine arts, and I like charitable causes; but you don't have to be a billionaire to be a patron. We're all patrons every day, and being a patron involves two choices, just like everything else: you can be fun, or you can be annoying.

Everyone dreams of being a "patron of the arts"; you know it's true, and you do. Wouldn't it be nice to just throw your money around for entertainment? The thing is, everyone is a patron; yes, we're all patrons of the arts. We buy music and video games; we go to movies, right? We all pay for entertainment. We all have power!

But so many people take their power for granted. So many people don't know how much power they have. And you know, most of the time they miss the art that's right in front of them!

My art was, and finally now again is, hospitality.

What is hospitality?

To quote Amy Sedaris, the author of *I Like You: Hospitality under the Influence*, "Whether you live in a basement with the income of a ten-year-old girl or on a saffron farm in the south of Spain, the spirit of hospitality is the same. It's the giving of yourself, a present of you to them from me to you."

Well, quoting successful authors might seem easy, but hospitality? Really? Really think it's easy? Try throwing a dinner party and get people to pay to attend.

Universities have degrees in hospitality. They give it fancy names like Restaurant and Hotel Management, and that makes it sound so easy.

Trust me, it's not easy; it's not something to be taken for granted.

Hospitality is theater but with the customer as a part of the act. You can rehearse all you want to, but nothing can really fully prepare you in advance to entertain people—people you don't know—unless you can think on your feet and communicate.

That's why I decided to study communications. I got my bachelor's degree in communications—paid for by bartending—and I wanted to teach it, so I was ready to get my master's degree and beyond. My goal was to help people learn how to do the most important thing in the world—get along with each other. I applied that every day, and I still do.

I was one hell of a bartender, and now I'm doing it again.

Why, all of a sudden, you might ask, is it a "was and now again is" thing?

Well, something happened, but I haven't let that stand in my way. You see, that's my nature. I don't let anything or anyone stand in my way.

Because of that, I have friends that respect me.

And hey, I've had a setback in life, but I haven't let that dampen my spirit; so why the hell should you?

"A setback you say? What was that?"

Well, there was this thing that happened.

One night I was driving home from work, when I suddenly found myself no longer driving home from work. Instead, I was in a strange, dark place, cut off from the world and without a clue as to how I got there.

I'm told that an unsecured piece of furniture flew off a rented trailer ahead of me in traffic and that it crashed through the windshield of my Jeep Liberty. The damage to my Jeep was extensive, but that's just glass and steel, and things can be fixed or, if necessary, replaced.

However, as you can imagine, my head didn't react so well to the flying debris. The resulting injuries to my skull, eyes, and face were the worst Seattle's Harborview Hospital's trauma center had ever seen. The rate of my blood loss was so severe that replacing it simply couldn't keep up. They induced hypothermia (chilling my body to slow down my body's need for oxygen), trying desperately to keep me alive. After doing everything they could and using the best judgment possible, they deemed my injuries to be terminal. They sent my family and friends home. Then began warming my body up in preparation for organ donation.

At that point—so I'm told—I reached out into the darkness and pushed the nurse's arm away.

What's happened since is a story I want to share with you. It's a story of a long, long road of recovery involving many surgeries. It's a story of relearning to talk, relearning to walk, and even relearning to think and to reason.

But it's more than that; those are just the technical details of my journey. The real story I want to share with you is how I gathered the strength to move forward, without anger and with hope for the future, and my determination to get back to life.

Of course, life is a chain of events forged one link at a time. It has a beginning, and it goes on until the end. Sure, you can look at a link in a chain, or several of them for that matter. That tells you about that particular link or set of links, but if you really want to know about it, you have to look at the whole chain.

So as they say, let me begin at the beginning.

LET ME BEGIN
AT THE BEGINNING

My grandfather worked in a bank. He knew the value of money, and he tried to teach me that. Every time he gave me a present, he'd wrap in it dollar bills all taped together.

It might sound strange to you, but there was a lesson in that: I didn't just tear into the presents I was given; I carefully unwrapped each one, knowing that the paper each present was wrapped in was worth something. I'd carefully unwrap each present, peeling the tape that held the dollar bills together wrapping them, because even though I was only four years old, I understood that a dollar was worth something and that the present inside was worth something. So I'd peel the dollars apart and arrange them just so and then, only then, would I open my present.

I wonder if you ever thought of it that way. After all, it takes money to buy presents. It even takes money to buy wrapping paper.

I'm sure that was his point.

I remember his house in Lincoln Park. I remember going to Grandpa and Grandma's house and how we'd eat the dinners she'd prepare around a table that seemed so big when I was a child. Of course, I remember playing there, under their watchful eyes. Oh, and the hot tub! What a wonder that was!

Of course, things happen. Life can be full of wonderment, and life can be treacherous. I also remember my first trip to the emergency room because I had run into the stairs instead of up them. So many stitches!

And of course other things happened—a dislocated shoulder, ear infections. As a result, there were more trips to the emergency room.

But I was a kid. I was a little girl. I was even Grandpa's little girl. So of course it was really about My Little Pony. Yeah, I did that. And I did the Cabbage Patch doll thing. And of course, there was Barbie.

Of course, we all grow up. So not much later in life, yet still as a little girl, my grandfather taught me about math. I remember going into my grandfather's office as he was writing things. I got in and sat on his knee as he worked. I loved him; he was my grandpa, and he loved me; I was his granddaughter. So I asked what he was doing, and he told me. And he taught me.

He taught me about math. Not in the usual sense, but the way that math was important to him. This is a one. This is a five. This is a ten. This is a twenty. Yes, I know this can all sound superficial. It's all about money, you might think, but it wasn't that way at all. He was wise enough to use things I'd seen in order to make math understandable. There are five ones in a five; there are two fives in a ten; there are two tens in a twenty. He was a banker, and he used what he knew to teach me about math.

There were other things I learned as I sat on his knee. I learned about the budget. I learned about the agenda. Every morning in his office, he made a plan: "What are we going to do today? What are we going to have to spend in order to do that?" I remember him saying. He always spoke of "the agenda" and "the budget." It was his way of trying to impart what he had learned from life on to the ones he loved.

And of course, there was always the "Twenty-Dollar Thing." He didn't do it all the time—as much as he wanted to spoil his granddaughter, and what grandfather wouldn't? Of course he wanted to spoil his grandchildren, but he did it with knowledge and experience, and the experiences he could create for us. He saved "The Twenty-Dollar Thing" for some special event or another. The "Twenty-Dollar Thing" was always special. It was a real event.

Of course, I could tell when it was going to happen. There would be that grin on his face before he would announce it. Kids know these sorts of things. They notice. Adults can't really hide things from kids—as much as they'd like to try.

So my grandfather had the "Twenty-Dollar Thing," not just for me, of course, but for all his grandchildren. I know I'm not special. I know I'm not the only one he tried to teach, but he sure made me feel that way.

Anyway, I'm sure you're wondering what the "Twenty-Dollar Thing" was—even though I'm sure you've kind of guessed. Well, of course, he'd proudly announce it, and then we'd go to the store and get anything and everything that twenty bucks could buy.

The nice thing about that was that it wouldn't be just twenty bucks of nonsense. I knew better than that. I knew about "the agenda." I knew about "the budget." And of course, you know that I knew then that I had a sense of when this was going to happen. So I went and simply spent it on stuff because I had a huge amount of money in my hand. I went shopping with a purpose. I had a plan. And I knew the value of what I was going to purchase.

My grandfather is a wise man.

I'm not from a rich family. I've lived a pretty much ordinary life. Because of that, simple things can appear to be spectacular to me, even today. I remember that my grandparents lived in a house with a large live-in, furnished basement. Their house was on a hill, so even the basement had windows overlooking a modest view, which was and is still wonderful to behold. But one of the most amazing things I remember was Christmastime, when they put up a tree in that basement. I remember that I'd never seen so many presents in my life! There were so many that it made the tree look not as big as it had when we first put it up. So many presents! And each with a lesson, outside and in.

Of course, there was Easter too. Easter at my grandparents' house was always a big event and lots of fun. My grandfather had taken out the grass in the front yard and replaced it with AstroTurf so that he could have a year-round nine-hole putting green. So when it came time to hunt for Easter eggs, I always remembered to check each of the holes for treasure. I remember it was fun to find the colored hard-boiled eggs, but I didn't care very much for hard-boiled eggs themselves—yuck! Finding candy was fun too. But there were also the special plastic Easter eggs with money inside. I really liked finding those!

My great-grandma lived on Lake Tapps, and I remember that we'd go there as well on Easter for picnics. It was fun to get dressed up for Easter in my pretty little dresses and go see my great-grandma. There was one year in particular that I decided that I wanted to choose my own hairstyle, so I picked a bowl cut. It was horrendous! But I picked it, so I was stuck with it. I still shudder and laugh at myself when I think about that fashion faux pas.

I have so many fond memories of family events. I remember fishing and clam-digging with my grandparents. I remember the chart with all the gold stars that I earned for doing the things I was supposed to do. I remember my uncle Bobby's wedding in Lincoln Park.

As I got older, I would go visit my dad. He lived in faraway exotic places—or so they seemed to me as a kid. I got to spend Christmases and summers in different states and places, including Alaska, California, and Hawaii. Even the different places in Washington state seemed far away and exotic.

I remember my first time visiting my dad in Alaska—there was this snow thing. I didn't know what that was about! And I got to watch a scary movie with him. I still can't swim in the ocean because of that! Yes, the movie was *Jaws*, and I don't like swimming in pools either. When I was a kid, I was so afraid that Jaws was going to burst through the side of the pool! I saw all kinds of scary movies as a kid, but Jaws is the only one that ever really, really scared me!

Of course, there were things in my life that people think of as scary, but I met those challenges head-on. A lot of people are afraid of doing something in front of other people. Most adults are afraid of talking in front of a crowd. How horrified would you be now if you were asked to be on stage and required to speak in front of a bunch of people? I'm guessing you'd get a lump in your throat, as the old expression goes. And what if you were expected to sing? What if you were expected to dance?

When I was five years old, my cousin Kristina was about two and a half. Kristina and I decided—well, I'm guessing it was more my idea than hers, given our ages at the time—to put on a show. We decided to put on a dance show for my grandparents. We had it all planned out. We went to a room far away from the family event that was going on, and we choreographed a little show.

When we were ready, I told my grandpa it was time, and he proudly announced that we were going to perform for everyone's enjoyment!

The stage was set. Okay, the stage was the hearth of the fireplace in my grandparents' living room, but it was our stage, our theater. It didn't matter that the orchestra was a tape player. The most important thing was that everyone had front-row seats, and everyone in the front row was important. So Kristina and I did our dance, and we bowed and smiled when they gave us a rousing round of applause.

Of course, as I mentioned, our dance shows were prepared in advance. We were serious about our performances. Kristina and I rehearsed. There were dance steps involved. I know; I was not only the producer, I was also the choreographer. I'm not sure how I felt about it then, but it makes me smile to remember how I wanted us to jump during part of our performance. Kristina wanted to do her best, and she tried so hard to do what I envisioned: I wanted us to jump as part of the dance, and she was so cute! First she'd bend her knees, then she'd get all focused and prepared, squatting down, all ready to go, and then she'd "jump"—she'd quickly stand up straight, her feet remaining firmly on the ground the whole time.

She thought she'd done it, and I didn't tell her differently. After all, she was two and a half, and I was five, and we were having fun. That was the point.

Of course, life isn't all fun and games. I knew that then, and I know that now. I've always thought about things. I like to ponder how to do things, how things work, how to get things done.

I took piano lessons. I got good at it. I hated it, but I made sure of that by following through.

In school, I was very focused. I always raised my hand. I almost always knew the answer. Even if I wasn't sure, I wasn't afraid to say what I thought I knew; because even if I was wrong, I always knew that I'd know a little more. I don't know how I got so many answers right, but I think this was how I did it. What I do know is that there was only one letter that I wanted to see on my papers, and that was the letter *A*.

One day, some boy walked up to me while I was playing with one of the girlfriends. He was walking by, and he stopped, and he put his hand on my forehead and slammed my head back against the brick wall of the school. I remember a lot of blood and that the teacher in charge of recess had to go get towels. What was that about? I didn't know. I didn't understand why that happened. I didn't understand why that was necessary.

I had a babysitter before and after school. She would give me an after-school snack. It was always cup-o-noodles. In a word, yuck! She had two sons in their teens, and they had video games. I remember playing two of them: Super Mario Bros. and Tetris. When I played Super Mario Bros., I always picked Luigi. His little green outfit was cool, whereas Mario's red outfit, well, as Luigi might say, "No so much, eh?"

In elementary school, I had lots of little report things to do. I always focused on making everything just right, again aiming for that nice big letter *A*. I made that happen every time—or just about.

The worst part about elementary school was gym class. I hated gym. If gym had been about exercise, I might have been interested in it; but it was always about really stupid, fake sports like dodgeball. I always thought I was going to get hurt; didn't see the point of it.

For a while, we lived with a friend who had a horse ranch. Being a kid, it was all fun and excitement—even getting the manure out of the stalls was fun for me. I like a tidy barn!

Then we moved into my grandparents' summerhouse, a private little lake cabin. For a while, I was still going to Kennydale Elementary, but when I turned ten, I changed schools to one much closer. I finally got to meet all the kids in my neighborhood, riding the bus to school.

I enjoyed making things habitable in the lake cabin, and I kind of felt like a housewife even though I was only ten years old. My mom left me on my own a lot and never made me breakfast, and school lunches were pretty disgusting. Fortunately, a girl a couple of houses away on the way to the bus had Nutri-Grain bars and Capri Sun foil packets, so at least there was that to look forward to! And what did I do after school? Well, I'd get home, turn on the TV, and do my homework, usually enjoying some Cool Ranch Doritos. Then I'd clean the house and make dinner for my mom. When she got home, she would eat, and then I'd go to bed.

Once we moved to that cabin, when I was about eleven, I got my first dog, a German shorthaired pointer. I named him Artie. I was the happiest I'd ever been. He'd walk with me to the bus stop, and he'd always be waiting for me at the bus stop after school, and we'd walk home together. He was the coolest dog ever.

I loved fishing, and we had a rowboat. I would row all the time all over the lake. I would pretend I was an explorer on the high seas, discovering new lands. There was also a floating dock. I remember I would take a couple of slices of bread and feed three ducks that lived there. One was black, one was white, and one was a mallard. I named them Larry, Mo, and Curly. They'd let me pick them up and carry them around like babies.

My uncle Richard built a set of monkey bars to play gymnast on. I had hours of fun on those bars, swinging and hanging from them, pretending I was in the Olympic Games.

Then there were my birthdays. My aunt Liz, the youngest of my grandpa's kids, would always throw me birthday parties from the time I was about age seven or so. I remember we'd have slumber parties, and we would watch movies. One time we watched *Halloween*. That was f—ing scary, and I loved it!

I started staying weekends with my aunt Liz and Uncle Steve too. Aunt Liz and Aunt Susan introduced Kristina and me to a wonderful phenomenon: we'd go shopping at the Mother Ship, as they called it, Nordstrom. Liz was working there as a manager, and she taught Kristina and me all about shopping or, as we called it, retail therapy. It was glorious!

Aunt Liz also introduced Kristina and me to another catchphrase reserved for people with absolutely no fashion sense whatsoever: "They deserve to be issued a fashion citation." Oh, how I regret how often I've felt it necessary to use that phrase under my breath to a friend. I mean, really, you don't have to look like you just walked out the pages of *Cosmo* or *Vogue*, but really, at least try to be presentable, people! Take at least a little pride in your appearance, will you?

My aunt Susan and her husband had a billiard parlor, and she'd let Kristina and me help with the bookkeeping. Then we mastered running the till, and we'd help out by getting customers their cues and balls and chalk, restocking the soda machine, and whatever else needed doing. We felt like

real businesspeople! It was very fun, and it's very funny to think b?
very serious we were about doing a good job.

I spent a lot of weekends with Aunt Susan and Uncle Richard. They had
Great Danes; but one day, we went to the airport, and we picked up this little
dog named Brewster. Playing with Brewster was the beginning of my love
and infatuation with Jack Russell terriers.

In grade school, I was in a split-level third- and fourth-grade class. Even
though I was a third grader, I was studying at the fourth-grade level. By the
time I got to fourth grade, I got an unwelcome surprise. All of a sudden,
before any of the other girls, I had to start wearing a training bra. A training
bra? Really? In the 1980s? One word comes to mind: irritating!

Then there was fifth grade. The most memorable thing about that was
having to take sex ed. We were learning about puberty and this period thing,
and in the midst of that, I went to the bathroom—oh no! I'm only ten years
old! That's not supposed to happen yet! At least that's what they told us! Got
that wrong, didn't ya!

I had braces for a while. I hated them. Fortunately, I didn't have to wear
the headgear to school and look like a nerd, but I did have to wear it at night.
Hated it, hated it, hated it!

I also had a boyfriend in the fifth grade. His name was Adam. We
"dated," but all that dating meant then was that we talked on the phone a lot
and smiled at each other in school.

Then sixth grade came along, middle school. I learned about cliques, and
I learned that I didn't care much about gossip. Cliques didn't seem that cool. I
was just into getting really good grades and stuff like that.

I wasn't into after-school sports or anything like that. I don't know if I
would have, and guess I'll never know; I was still stuck being a "housewife."
My mom worked full-time, and when she'd get home, she'd go to the barn
and ride her horse for a couple hours. Then she'd eat the meal I'd cooked
for her, and then she'd go to bed. No after-school activities for me; I was too
busy having to cook, clean the house, feed the dog and the cats, and take care
of her.

Once a week, I'd be driven to the Laundromat. Here I was, just a kid,
doing all the laundry by myself at ten years old; but I knew if my mom had
done it, it would have been all wrong—whites with colors and things all
folded wrong. I wasn't going to live like that—that's for sure!

By the seventh grade, I'd pretty much gotten the hang of middle school.
I got interested in math and science and excelled at them. I guess that goes
back to my grandfather making math interesting to me as a little girl.

In the eighth grade, the clique thing really kicked in. All the popular girls
turned on me. I'm not sure why they did that, but I certainly was shocked at

how rude and bitchy they became. I guess it might have been that I always did my own thing. I remember I took a picture from a teen magazine to a hairstylist, thinking the model looked cute; afterward, I decided short hair didn't look so good on me. That was one of the many things they picked on me about.

But the heck with them. I decided to become friends with a different girl, and we got along great. For our eighth-grade science project, we decided to test which hair spray had the most hold. So we washed our hair, dried it, and then hair-sprayed our bangs straight up. We measured the height of our bangs. Then we rode down a hill on our bikes as fast as we could and measured them again. Then we washed, dried, and moved on to the next hair spray we wanted to test. Not only did we have fun, we got great grades too!

Of course, I still hated gym class. It was still pretty much a waste of time. The gym teacher was horrible! I was so glad when I learned that there was a way I could get out of it though. So I joined the National Junior Reserve Officer Training Corps, or NJROTC. That took care of that problem. Four months in ninth grade.

Just when I had everything pretty well worked out and had school down to a science, my mom got a job transfer—to Utah. Ugh! I didn't like the weather. I didn't like it one bit. Also, ninth grade in Utah meant I got pushed back into junior high school. I didn't like that very much; I was ready to be in high school! And the clothes! Oh my god, the clothes! I liked wearing what was cool, new, and trendy; but looking around me, all I could think was that I felt like 1985 should call and ask for their look back!

As I said, in Utah, junior high school ran through the ninth grade, so I got shoved back into junior high. I got great grades, but the classes were a lot easier than the honors classes I had been taking in Seattle. The math curriculum was about as advanced, but everything else was as much as two years behind what I had been used to. So it was a breeze, but it was also boring, boring, boring, and it drove me nuts.

I did meet one nice girl there who was cool. I visited her house. She had something on her bedroom wall that made me think she was even cooler: a poster of Kurt Cobain! This was just after he had passed away. Compared to everyone else I met in Utah, she was pretty awesome.

At least they had a Nordstrom! So I got a job there. It gave me my roots back to Seattle and made me feel a little less homesick. I also worked at a neat clothing store called Mr. Rags.

The summer before I turned sixteen, I visited my dad in Alaska. I was amazed how it was light all the time. It was strange not to have nighttime. My dad has always been into weight lifting and bodybuilding, so I went to the gym with him. Working out made me feel good. I learned to like exercise, and it made me wonder why we hadn't done that in gym class! I'm still not into sports, but I love a good workout.

My dad has a PhD in psychology, so we always talked about meaningful stuff while I was there. And I got to drive his car. Now that was fun!

Of course, having a father with a PhD in psychology can be helpful in this crazy world.

About two weeks before I turned sixteen, I started dating my friend's boyfriend's older brother. I hadn't even French-kissed a guy at that point in my life. The tongue thing sounded disgusting! Then all of a sudden, I did it all. A few weeks later, I couldn't figure out why I was vomiting all the time. I ended up going to Planned Parenthood. Oh, the protestors! Don't they have a clue? Don't they understand what can happen to a girl? I'm thinking that they don't even bother to think about it or ever put themselves into a person's shoes.

When I was a toddler, there was a teenage boy that I used to play with. He would roughhouse, and one time he dislocated my shoulder. I remember that he took me into a room and stuck something in me, and I just knew that it hurt, and he kept doing it. Little kids, when something like that happens to them, don't tell because they don't know that anything happened. I was confused when it happened and began to understand it when I started to learn about sex. I told my mom a few years later, and she didn't believe me; she said I was just lying. My dad, on the other hand, was understanding and compassionate. He told me that most people that have something like that happen to them don't usually begin to deal with it until they're well into their twenties. My dad's a pretty cool guy.

Anyway, after my visit to Alaska, it was back to Utah. Increasingly, I didn't like school. When I started my senior year, the first couple of months were horrible. I found the education system in Utah to be lacking in many ways. In general, it simply didn't provide any sort of intellectual challenge for me. I didn't want to get set back when it came time for me to go to college. So right before Christmas vacation, I went to talk to a guidance counselor. I told the counselor that I really wanted to be in college right then because the high school program wasn't doing anything to advance my education. So I arranged to graduate early, and I immediately enrolled in the winter and spring quarters at Weber State University in 1998. What a relief it was to actually be learning again!

Soon after that, I returned to Seattle. Things were much better for me. Much better. I set my sights on attending the University of Washington, but I knew I'd have to wait a year to qualify as in state. I always thought that was strange, since most of my life, I'd lived in Washington. You'd think that if you spent a lot of years as a resident, that would count for something. Nope. Had to wait a year. So I did.

While I was waiting on that nonsense, I decided to start making money for school. I decided to get a job at Nordstrom; after all, what better place to work than the "Mother Ship"? Not to mention that this would allow me to get some "retail therapy" with an employee discount!

Then I bought my first Jeep—a brand-new Jeep Wrangler with a soft top. Of course it was black; is there any other color for a Jeep? I think not! And of course, I had to dress it up, so I ordered aftermarket steps and bumpers for it. I got the cool tubular ones, which made it look really rugged and sexy. I was proud of myself too because I installed the steps and bumpers myself!

In preparation for college, I had already tried some career-related jobs to see what I might be interested in pursuing at UW. In Utah, I had worked at a chiropractic clinic, I had taken classes to become a phlebotomist, and I had considered nursing school. After returning to Seattle, I did some work for a couple of attorneys. I also interned at the Seattle Municipal Court, filing paperwork and learning more about our legal system—sometimes more than I wanted to know, since the area I worked in dealt with abuse cases.

One day, I got a surprise letter. It was a scholarship to UW, paying for a third of my tuition for the first two years! So I enrolled and took some general-requirement classes. I took a psychology class, which was interesting; but I'd already had enough experience with that due to my dad. Then I took a speech communications class and found I really liked that. So I enrolled in speech communications, and I got an internship with KJR Sports Radio and got to go to lots of events and set things up.

Then I turned twenty-one, and a whole new world opened up for me. As part of a KJR promotion involving a girl calendar, I was at Belltown Billiards and decided to apply for a job. The owner hired me on the spot. I started front desk. Then I spent a year cocktailing, and then I moved on to bartending. I thought it was interesting that, among other things, here I was, back to handing out pool balls again!

It was interesting to be a cocktail server. Working in crowds of people with a tray of drinks over my head, I got to see a lot of things. It was interesting to see people go from acting fine and normal then, an hour later, like idiots. And let me tell you, there are a lot of bad dancers out there! So I trained for bartending. It was a relief to get away from the crowd and have a bar between me and the customers—not in general, but it sure was nice to have something between me and the bad ones!

I got a job at Tini Bigs, which featured martinis, cocktails, and cigars. I enjoyed working around a more mature crowd. I liked snipping cigars and lighting them for the customers and having the time to have an actual conversation with them as part of the scene. I also got work as a VIP bartender at Medusa, which was a dance club with a lot of energy. I enjoyed the social aspect of it all, although I could have done without some of the drama!

When I turned twenty-two, I moved out on my own. I became roommates with a fellow cocktail server at Belltown Billiards. It felt good to be out on my own, totally self-reliant. I worked and paid for school and clothes. Of course, I kept driving Jeeps, since there is no better vehicle in my opinion. I traded in my Wrangler for a new black Jeep Liberty.

During that whole time, I was very serious about college. I only had two quarters without a full load. My life was all about school, work, and commuting. I still managed to work in a social life and dating. I didn't have any sort of regular schedule, so I had to catch some sleep when I could, which didn't happen as often as I would've liked! But I'm the sort of person who likes to just do things and take on all challenges; I never let challenges take me!

I finished school, graduating with honors. I really liked school, so I filled out an application for graduate school to get a master's degree in communications. My long-term goal had become to get a PhD in communications and to become a professor. I moved into my own apartment in Renton and started saving up money for graduate school and to make a down payment on a house of my own.

My new apartment was a little studio. It was the first time I'd lived anywhere that had a dishwasher. I bought a butcher-block roll-away island from IKEA for the tiny kitchen.

I have cleanliness issues; I like things to be neat and tidy. So even in my apartment's walk-in pantry, I organized everything. Even the canned goods were organized by type, which now I realize prepared me well for the blind lifestyle I have to lead today.

In my new apartment, I enjoyed cooking in my own kitchen. Because school was done for the time being, I also enjoyed being able to sleep on a more regular schedule, although it was service-industry schedule. As a result, I would occasionally meet up with friends with similar hours, have a bite to eat, talk, and have fun. My life took on a rhythm of grocery shopping, cleaning my apartment, working out, and finally getting decent sleep! I was still busy bartending, so I didn't have time for much else.

Before I moved to Renton, I had lived in Kirkland for a little while. While I was there, I started working at a restaurant with a bar on the waterfront called the Foghorn, serving and bartending. There I met my friend Mason, and we became best buddies. He was and still is like a brother to me.

I don't remember anything about the night of my accident. What I know about that night is what Mason told me. According to him, it was a typical night. We closed up the restaurant, did our side work and cleaned, counted the tills, and sat down and had our shift meal—an entrée and a glass of wine. We said our good-byes, and I climbed into my black Jeep Liberty, not knowing that my life was about to change dramatically and forever.

Uncle Bobby

There are a lot of things I don't remember because of what happened to me. A big chunk of wood flew through my windshield, and I took a hit in the face that a prizefighter couldn't take. The best medical minds available were ready to give me up for dead.

But I survived.

Sure, there are pieces of my life that are missing, but I beat the expectations of everyone around me: the professionals, my friends, and even my family.

What happened to me created gaps in my memory. There is a bit in the middle that's missing, but there are people that can fill in the gap. Fortunately, I have people that knew me then and know me now. People that I trust and who mean a lot to me.

In order to tell you what I've been through, I have to rely, in part, on the memory of others. So I decided to get together with the people that are closest to me in order to fill in the gaps.

One of those people is my uncle Bobby. He knows me well. He's a college professor. He teaches at Olympic College and does research at the University of Washington. When I was a kid, he taught me a lot of things, and he's always been a big part of my life. He is my grandparents' third child, the first and only boy, and was named after his dad, my grandfather. He is always reading—in the car, at breakfast—face always in a book. He is always going to school and is book smart. He always smiles. He is always doing things for other people and is always helping, from weeding to oyster hunting. I guess that's why he became a professor and likes to teach. He is a father of two boys; his wife is Kim. Tall and lean, all he does is ride his bike. His chestnut hair is thick and wavy, and his eyes deep in thought.

So on a bright summer's day I decided to ask him to meet me at the Bridge—our local watering hole—where I'd been tending bar again for the first time after all these years.

The first question I had was, "What is your earliest memory of me?"

Bobby responded, "The first time I saw you was on your birthday. You were born on Whidbey Island, and Kim and I weren't married yet, and we were still in college, and we drove up to Whidbey Island and saw you and held you that day. Kim and I would come up to Whidbey Island, and we'd spend a couple nights. We helped your dad with the log cabin he was building. I remember that we had to get you goat's milk every morning because you were allergic to cow's milk, and so we'd go to the farm, and we'd take you along. You were a little ways away up in Whidbey Island, but we'd get up there to visit you.

"And of course you were at our wedding. That was in September, so you were just shy of two years old at the time. Joe brought you to our wedding, right?"

"Yeah, he did," I said, thinking of the wedding pictures at Lincoln Park. I love that park, and I used to go there all the time with my grandparents. And I cringed to think of the awful haircut I had at the time!

"So let's see," he continued. "That was '81, and actually, we saw quite a bit of you, because you spent a lot of time with my mom."

That triggered a flood of memories, so I started with the first one. "Oh yeah, I remember how she taught me about the potty-chair and about getting a gold star on my chart if I went in it. Yeah!" The chart was kept on the refrigerator door, and on it was a record of everything I did right, such as following the rules and learning how to do things.

Bobby chuckled, and continued, "Yeah. About that time, Kim was in her second year of law school, and I moved down to Portland with her. We'd just get up and see you once in a while then, and we didn't get back up here until '83 when I was going to school until we left for LA in '87 . . ."

"Yep!" I confirmed.

"So we'd see you a lot during that time," he continued. "Was that when you lived on Lake Kathleen? If you were out at Lake Kathleen, then . . ."

I thought for a moment, and said, "Not quite."

"Not quite out there yet. No, you were . . ." He trailed off in thought for a second, and then inquired, "Where were you living then? I can't remember where the heck you were!"

"I think we were living at the horse ranch," I said.

"Then we were still in Seattle," he said, as the order of events came back to him. "And we saw quite a bit of you then. It was after we moved to

LA that you moved to Lake Kathleen. We'd come out and see you in the summers, and you'd come down to visit us in LA."

Another flood of memories came into my mind. "I remember that you'd help me with my ninth-grade calculus," I recalled. "I remember that when I stayed with you guys."

"Yeah, I probably was able to help you with your math," Bobby said modestly.

"Yes!" I said, laughing. "Since my uncle teaches physics and astronomy!" I couldn't see it, of course, but I could sense that he was smiling.

Changing the subject back to me, he continued, "Yeah, and then we came back to Seattle, and I'd see you quite a bit, because Lake Kathleen was still swimmable. I mean, I love my family, but I really love Lake Kathleen! I could swim in it from when I was a kid, and until I was forty-five, I swam in Lake Kathleen. I did it until it wasn't a lake anymore. You get a certain amount of ear infections, and you think, 'Yeah, it's over.'"

I laughed. You see, Lake Kathleen is a fairly shallow lake, and it gets comfortably warm in the summer; but since it's shallow, it also has a lot of brown silt that gets stirred up. The silt can get all over you, and you end up looking like you got a really bad fake tan. I remembered it was so bad that Bobby would hose himself off after a swim.

Then I remembered my dog Arthur—Artie for short—and how he loved to swim. Artie and I loved jumping off the dock into the lake. I tried that with the cat one time, but the cat didn't like it much. That cat practically walked on water as he swam to get out of the lake! I remembered putting a mattress on the end of the dock, with a little bit of it hanging over the end. I'd get it all wet with the hose, and then run down the dock, flop on the mattress, and slide off the dock, belly flopping into the lake. I also liked to row and was "master of the rowboat," and I loved to go fishing and catch trout. And oh, how the sound would carry so easily over the water! You could hear people's dogs barking so far away. In the winter, we'd go walking on the ice.

Bobby continued, drawing me back from memory lane, "Even when you moved away, you'd come back to the lake a lot, so I'd see you quite a bit. You were in your apartment for about three or four months, six months?"

"Yeah," I confirmed. "About six months. Something like that. But I liked how you helped me figure things out."

"And I never saw your apartment later until I helped move you out of it after your wreck," Bobby said.

"And oh, that night," he continued. "We got the call, and it was after midnight I'm sure. I don't remember the times anymore, but it was in the morning, and I was on my way in about eight minutes. I drove down to the hospital, and I took Kim's cell phone, and as I drove, I called Kim, and she guided me the rest of the way, using her computer so I could just get there faster. The important thing was to get on the road. And I came in, and I went in to see you. You were in ER, and they had your head completely wrapped, and I sat . . ."

Then he paused. It was a huge pause. I felt him grab into one of the boards of the picnic table, and I could hear the boards of the table creak a little.

Bobby continued, with a lot of obvious strain in his voice, "And I sat on your right side, and I held your hand. The person that was there in the emergency room . . . You were bleeding pretty well, and I sat down—I mean—I just sat down. I grabbed a chair, and I sat down next to you, and you were lying there, and I put my hand in yours. And, uh . . ."

Another long pause. It was clear that his emotions were welling up without being able to see him.

"And the intern . . . the uh . . . I don't know what he was, probably a nurse—I'm sure he was a nurse—he was very nice, and he told me there simply wasn't anything they could do. You were just bleeding out too much. And I could—from what I saw, they couldn't contain it all. So I . . . there was nothing I . . . you know how I am. I'm not real smart, but I can show up, so I just sat there, and I held your hand. For quite a while. At some point, I don't know who was out there, but they wanted me to come out and say something—you know, just talk—and so I went out . . . and there was blood on my shoes, that's how bad you were bleeding, and I wiped that off, and I talked to them, and they took you upstairs, and really they were just trying to—ah! They really weren't sure what to do, you were just bleeding too much, and there was nothing—they couldn't sew up enough things, so they took you upstairs.

"By that time Kristina was there, Suzy was there, Charlie was there, Richard was there . . . I imagine Lizzie was there . . . I'm sure, man, the whole family converged, and they asked your mom to sign an organ-donor card, and they were trying to keep you hydrated long enough so they could save your organs. They asked a bunch of questions, and I remember Kristina was there helping out with that.

"And then there was nothing that could really be done. I drove your mom home because she couldn't be driving. We stopped and got coffee, and none of us had money, but your mom had your handbag and said this would be good karma, so she paid with some of the money you had, and I gave that money back to you about three years later. I kept your things in a closet, and I never even looked to see how much money was in there . . ."

After he said that, I reached for my handbag and pulled out my favorite Coach wallet. "It's right here!" I said, holding it out to him. "That's what you gave me back!"

I'm sure he smiled at that, and then he said, "So we went home, and I took a shower, and then I went to school. I had a morning class and an afternoon class, and I taught those. And in between classes, they called to say you'd moved your hand, that they tried to do something and you brushed them away! By that time, my mother and father were up here from Las Vegas, and there was a four-ten ferry, so left my class about five minutes early, and I rode down to the ferry. As I was getting on the ferry, I saw Kim was in a car with my parents, and they were in the front of the line to get on, so we wound up all going together. Aunt Dolores and Uncle Bill were there, Aunt Bid and Andre . . . just all kinds of family showing up for you. And you know, this went on for weeks.

"Then it was just a waiting game. You survived, and they did multiple surgeries. It was a Sunday night, so that was Monday morning, and by Thursday or Friday, they'd done the operations, and it was massive. You were in for . . . It was about a fourteen-hour operation as I recall. And your face, they had to do that completely from photographs. It was like papier-mâché. They put titanium pieces in you that plagued you for years, because sometimes they'd change as you regrew, and they'd hurt a lot, so you'd have to rework them. And they used some bone from your hip, as I recall. And they reconstructed your face from pictures, and they had to get pictures of you from different angles to put you back together. And then, I don't know how long you were there, and I saw you a lot. You didn't know where you were . . ."

"What were the things I said?" I asked.

Bobby laughed a bit nervously. "I'm not gonna repeat some of them, but it was a couple of weeks before they took the tracheostomy tube out. Before that, they didn't really know what was there.

"There was a night when we danced. You were moving and really wanted something to do, so we danced. And we really didn't know what was inside. I'd walk you on a regular basis and, oh, my mother! My mother was there—in her midseventies she lived there, spent the nights—and I'll tell ya, you fell down one night, and she threw herself under you to protect you. And in your head you thought she pushed you down, and you hated her for months, and oh my god, that hurt her. There was nothing, and you didn't have any choice, you didn't know, and it was so hard for her. But you know, a brain injury, right? When you could talk, we figured out it was like—I think it was when you first could talk, and this was two or three weeks after, and you could keep track of things for about a minute or two, and then you'd repeat—which was great, because none of my stories got old!

"So we'd talk to you, and we'd spend, and there was somebody there every night with you—I'm guessing for the first month or two. And the hospital staff couldn't do it, so we did. So mostly it was Mom. Suzy and everybody else were so helpful. Suzy did stuff and Liz too.

"Then there was the jumble of trying to figure out the financial aspects of it all! There was a guy, and I have his card. He worked there at Harborview, and he was incredible. And he took us through it, and he did a much more important job back somewhere in Asia, like Vietnam, and he came over here and he was doing this, and he's one of the people that saved your lifestyle so you could get through to where you are now.

"So it got better. You did have to go to the bathroom every two minutes, it seemed, so I took you to the bathroom every two minutes, and you would forget where you were. I'd take you for a walk throughout the hospital—and keep in mind, I'm working, and other people in my family were doing far more hours. Of course they weren't doing like me, riding a bike up that hill to the hospital! But everybody in the hospital knew you. I'd take you to a bathroom on some floor we'd never been to, and people that were cleaning up the area said hi to you. They knew about you. You weren't supposed to live.

"And from there, you got moved to another place. All these people, so many people, came to see you from the family, and they were very supportive. And you know, I just thought people would get tired after a while, but they didn't.

"They moved you to another area in the hospital, and eventually, you moved to Good Samaritan. You'd call at about two a.m.—a lot. You had no sense of day or night, how would you? And by this time, it was every six minutes or eight minutes that you didn't know where you were, because the record would just keep replaying. So we'd just keep visiting, and eventually, I think by around June, you got out, and I drove you home.

"And everything hurt you. You were really uncomfortable driving . . ."

"Oh, I hated it!" I said. "Especially if it was someone driving a stick shift!"

"Oh, I was driving a stick shift, but you didn't mind," Bobby said.

I replied, "Well, you're a guy. You drive 'em better, let's just be honest."

Bobby continued, "So I took you home, and I guess for the next five years, I came every week. And the reason was, well, there's a lot of reasons. First, I wanted to be supportive. It was hell, you went through a lot of things. When you're brain damaged, there's range of emotions that you have no control over in the beginning—and you don't remember much of all that stuff, but there were a range of emotions that you went through, and nobody could really, well, it's difficult to . . . it's very difficult to picture, or even imagine, unless you're there. So part of it was to show my support, and part of it was you guys just got used to me being there every Saturday with coffee in hand.

"You wouldn't put a guard up. You know, when somebody comes for a visit, you're on your best behavior and stuff, and for me, I just kept showing up. I'd show up for an hour, sometimes two hours, but it was a regular thing, so I could just sort of get an idea of how you were doing. And you were getting better. A lot of people thought you were doing great, but I could see after . . . you know after about a half hour, the stories would repeat. You're great at impressing people, my gosh.

"But you'd get angry and frustrated. No shit, right? That's the part you read about brain trauma injuries with veterans—the violence, the emotions, the angst, and everything? You're not in control over those kind of things. And they just slowly improve."

Bobby was right about the symptoms, but it wasn't the whole story. Sure, I was pissed and felt like I wanted to explode, but it wasn't because I wasn't in control of my emotions. It was that no one else could see what was going on inside my head, and they just weren't getting it. Everyone's assumptions about what was going on with me were a misinterpretation of what was really going on.

Inside my head, everything was working fine. Everything was crystal clear. The problem was the disconnect between my brain and my ability to communicate. I was frustrated and angry because I was tired of saying one thing and hearing my mouth say something completely different. Oh, I'd get so pissed, for sure, but not for the reasons anyone thought! I didn't tell Bobby what was ticking over in my brain, but this time, it was because I was being polite instead of not being able to get it out.

Bobby went on, "In 2007, we cleaned up the house next door so that you could have your own place, and I spent a few weeks working there. I could see by that point people thought you were doing great, and you were. In relative terms you were doing great. By then, it was every two hours, every three hours things would repeat, and you couldn't go beyond that. It's just a wild thing. It was so tough for you, and it was so tough for the people around you. But a lot of great people came into your life at the right times to mentor you. You'd get tired of them at different points as you progressed, but each of them contributed to your rehabilitation to an incredible degree. And this worked really well for you.

"From the perspective of those around you, you're telling them the same things every two minutes, every five minutes, seven minutes, ten minutes, half hour, and you can get pissed at things. So it's a good thing to get new people in all the time that could take care of you in different ways. There were a lot of helpful things that happened. All the people caring for you hurt for you, but they also benefited from it at the same time. They could all see the results of what they did. They could see all the big improvements, and that was pretty great.

"So you got to live in your own house, and that got that separation going, and that was a huge thing because you got to live on your own, but you also had some safety. Eventually, then, you got to move out to your own place."

I thought about that for a moment, and then something occurred to me. "I remember when I first went out was a couple of months after I got home to Lake Kathleen, and my friends Marsala and Mason took me out to eat at Bahama Breeze."

Bobby responded cautiously, "You were very quiet. It was hard for you to get out."

I knew what he was saying, but being me, I of course responded, saying it plainly and clearly, "Yeah, I was quiet sometimes, and sometimes I wasn't. For instance, I remember I ordered a pasta. I was so pissed because I couldn't eat it normally because of my jaw. Oh, I was so pissed! I mean, I wasn't like swearing or whatever, but I was like, 'What the hell's going on here? What the hell's going on?' I remember that, and I remember a little later when my personal trainer Tracy took me out dancing one night, and that's when I really actually felt somewhat back to normal."

Bobby chimed in again, "I remember you went to a wedding, and you danced. That was early on."

"Well, the first wedding I went to—" I said. "Well, wait, what wedding was that . . . Oh, that was college friend Kristin! Yeah, that was early, because I was in the wedding. I was one of her bridesmaids in '04. I remember I was dancing, and that was fun. And then I remember going to another wedding back in '06. It was a girl I used to work with, Briana, and she married a guy that became her manager, and they got married, and the wedding was at Medusa—where my birthday party was. And Krysten Cook, who was taking care of me then, took me there. She and her husband, with my boyfriend at the time."

"You got into beads for a while," Bobby said. "You were selling beads at the farmers' market."

"Yeah," I said. "You know Krysten Cook, her dad is an art professor. Krysten was into beading, and she had me try it."

"So whatever was interesting to you, we pushed it," Bobby said. "About that time, people started speaking about secure loads. At first, you wouldn't say anything. And then it was like—I think it was the time down in downtown Seattle, at the 'Secure Your Load Campaign' at Qwest Field. Ron Simms and the King County prosecutor Norm Maleng and Dan Satturberg were there, and then you actually said something."

"And then you started . . ." he continued, his voice catching a bit on a welling-up of emotion. "You started opening up. It was like there were these hurdles that you had to get over, and, uh . . ."

Bobby trailed off, and I could feel he was at a loss for words, so I changed the subject slightly. "I didn't like going to the speaking engagements. I didn't mind when I was there. I'll tell you the worst part about them—driving there and driving back. Because my mom would play country music. My god!"

That lightened his mood. He laughed and said, "Yeah!"

I laughed with him, saying, "And I was listening to it, going, 'What the hell?'"

"Yeah." He chuckled. "That's hard to handle when it's not your kind of music!"

"All my exes live in Texas!" I sang with a drawl.

"And were sisters and brothers," he twanged back at me, and we laughed. With that little dose of laughter, he was able to continue. "We'd push things like that because we'd see you opening up. You know, speaking of opening up, there were the exercises to try to open your mouth. We tried to get you to see a dentist to do that."

"Riiiight . . ." I responded sarcastically to his pun.

He carried on, "And it was like always trying to figure out a path to get you out and open and to talk and stuff. You were very quiet, those talks about unsecured loads started bringing you out even though they were uncomfortable for you. But most things that improve you are uncomfortable. So there were a myriad of techniques people used that were just based on what was going on around you."

"They forgot one technique, though. Right here, in the glass," I said, pointing to my beer. "You know? It helps."

We laughed again, and he said, "I think you were on so many pills at the time, and you were dealing with all these infections as well. I mean, you had lots of issues. You've still got MRSA, I'm sure."

"Well, I've got pockets of it who knows where in my head," I said. "The doctors don't even know where all of it is."

"And congestion," he continued. "At the time, just about anything—and I don't know where you're at now, but at the time, just about anything could have killed you, right? I mean, they still don't really know what your physiology is. And so it's like every day, to me, every day is a gift, right? Your cardiovascular system has undergone such trauma and leaked in so many places. It's scarred, and it's a tough battle. You knew you had to take care of any kind of virus, any kind of bacterial infection could have been it. And what are you going to breathe through, right? So there were many moments of hell for you. And I got to come for an hour every Saturday or Sunday and then leave. For instance, you went through the big flu—"

"Oh, that was a pain in the ass!" I interjected. "Swine flu. That was a pain."

"But you pulled through it!" Bobby said.

"I beat a one-hundred-eight-degree fever, and I beat it within two days. It was gone!" I said proudly.

"You have a strong system." Bobby observed. "You passed pretty much the highest tests. The doctors don't know of anybody . . . they hadn't seen someone like you before when you got to Harborview. They were talking about taking you to Overlake, and if you'd gone to Overlake, you wouldn't have made it. It was a combination of you and the people available. You had some of the best people in the world, and they happened to be there."

"One day," I recalled, "I don't know why, I went to go find some of the medics. I found one of them in Auburn. He showed up at court. We went and sat down and visited with him. A lot of tears."

"That was huge," said Bobby. "The couple that found you after the accident, I'm sure that they're still feeling the effects."

"They should see me now!" I said confidently. "But I'm curious. What are your thoughts about me before the accident and me today?"

Bobby thought for a little bit. He drew a deep breath and finally said, "There's subtle differences. I'll tell ya, you know, you're still Maria, but there's certain things. You're not exactly the same person. Things had to rewire. So it's . . . I think that happens with every brain injury, and I learned that. You have to grieve for the person that was there before, there's some grieving that happens. And it's subtle. There's subtle differences. It's not exactly the same, you know?"

I chimed in, "A girl that worked here at the Bridge for a little bit, and now she's down at Salty's, Courtney, she used to work at the Frontier Room, which was the same owner that owned Belltown Billiards and Club Medusa, so I knew her since about a year after I started at Belltown Billiards. I was roommates with Marcella, and when Courtney moved out is when I moved in. Recently, she came to dinner at our house in West Seattle, and our friend Dave came and cooked. Courtney brought my friend John, who was in town visiting. I asked Courtney what I was like before and after the accident. Her response was that I'm not quite as snotty now!"

We both laughed. "That's funny!" Bobby said, and we laughed again.

"Uh-huh! I like that!" I said, tossing my head, putting on a little snotty attitude.

Bobby waxed analytical, "That's the interesting thing about a brain trauma injury, it's hard to pinpoint because there are just subtle differences.

It's not quite the same. The neural paths have to be completely regenerated in some cases. And so it's you, but it's different. A lot of what you went through has affected you, and I'm not . . . that's not why they call me a doctor, so I don't *know*. It's more an MD thing. It's a tricky thing. So as Crosby, Stills, Nash & Young said, 'Love the one you're with.'"

"Do you remember what the doctors said?" I asked. "Do you remember what they said my outcome would be? What did they say? What were their thoughts?"

"They didn't know," Bobby replied. "They really didn't know. They said . . . really they were guessing, but they were really up-front about it. They said you just don't know, and you see what happens. They said you had made great improvement so far, and we don't know where it'll stop. We don't really have a good idea of what the damage is. You know, the MRI gives you some information, but we don't know that much about the brain. You know, people go to doctors and expect pure science. There's science involved, but it's tough. There's so much we don't know. We have no appreciation of our own existence."

"Doctors mean well," I responded, "but they don't always know. They said I'd never open my mouth ever again. I still had this condition, and I had that condition, and they signed off, and that's that."

"There was a time where you just didn't want to mess with it," Bobby said. "I think part of it was you were just recovering from a lot of things—and it was still just a few years after that. Part of it may have been that you were ready to break free from your mom and stuff. But you didn't even want to look into the jaw surgery at the time. I think that's when you went, and you were finally ready for it. But there was an option—they didn't know what they could do, right?"

"Yes," I said. "Because even Dr. Hopper, after a certain point, said, 'This is where it is, we've done everything we can, and you just have to stretch out your jaw more.'"

"Well, they were trying to get you to stretch it out and everything, but you never quit on it, you just stopped." Bobby reflected. "You didn't like it. You just stopped on that. But we knew that you'd get there eventually, and you got there."

I continued, saying, "The doctor that did the surgery checked all the records, and he started prodding my face, and I'd flinch. When they look at that scan, it's a 3-D scan, and when you peel the skin away, there's no nerves. There's nothing. The doctor said I shouldn't be blinking, but I blink. The doctor goes, 'I don't know why you're blinking. It shouldn't be happening. And you flinch, and there's no nerves. I don't understand this.' That doctor did a nine-hour surgery on me to get my jaw to open again. He said, 'The thing we don't understand is the brain.' He also said he wasn't going to try to second-guess the brain. He said, 'It's working, so we're going to go with it.'"

Bobby replied, "You thought for several months that you could see, because what happens—I did some reading on this. One of the largest centers in our brain is the one that controls sight because it takes a lot of input and we use our sight just about more that any other perception. When you lose your sight, that part of the brain starts doing other things. So when you would reach out for something, you could 'see' it because your brain was translating. Your brain can't see things. It takes photons, and it turns it into something. But your brain would take it, and it would turn it into what it could see. So you could move your hand, and you could sort of see things with your hand."

Bobby paused again, deep in thought, and then blurted out, "I was just flashing back . . . Most of the time when we would sit and talk, I would close my eyes. After a while, I would just naturally do it so that I could be in the same world as you."

"You were always like that," I responded. "You have that thing where you put yourself in someone else's shoes in order to figure out how to help them."

He went on. "Anytime any of my nieces or nephews asked for help, they'd always get it. If you had trouble with anything in school, I was always able to help you with it."

"You helped me get whatever the teacher was saying by saying it in a way that made sense to me." I recalled.

Bobby replied, "Your decision-making skills were great. You rarely asked for help, and the few times you did, I was certainly happy to assist. All the kids in our family made good use of my willingness to help. But yeah, any help with school you needed, you always got. I guess I try to show people how to learn it for themselves."

"It's was the way the teachers were teaching it," I said. "A lot of times when it wasn't quite hitting me . . . One time, I was down to visit you in California for a week or so, and you helped me with a few things, and—"

"You were down twice, I remember," interjected Bobby, "because I remember I taught you how to shoot free throws there."

"I remember that!" I said, smiling at the thought of it.

"But you know the deal," Bobby said. "You can teach people a rule or something, or you can teach them how it works so they remember it."

I thought for a second or two and said, "It's neat that we had the kind of family that would help each other out with that kind of thing. A lot of times people just rely on the school system to do the whole job, but we really need people in our lives that do more than that."

I continued, "You helped me with precalculus, and a couple of years before that, you taught me the neat things I could do with the TI-87 calculator. You helped me figure a lot of stuff out."

"Oh, you'd figure it out," Bobby said, "because you're smart and real stubborn! Man, you have supreme confidence, and you were stubborn, and you thought you could do it better than everybody else, and I thought, 'That's gonna get her sometime,' but it saved your life. Really. I mean, you had to be real obstinate to make it through all the things you've had to go through, and that's what did it."

I replied, feisty as ever, "I wasn't gonna listen to any medical doctor that said I couldn't do this or would never do that, what the hell do they know?"

Bobby quipped, "Yeah, and there weren't any shamans around, so ..."

We both laughed.

Aunt Susan

My aunt Susan is a second daughter and a second child. She worked for American Airlines ticketing and baggage. When I was a kid, she rode and showed horses; these days, she rides Harleys and a Vespa. She loves dogs and takes great care of her pets. She introduced me to Jack Russell terriers. Susan is the mother of my first cousin, Kristina. Organization, order, and great fashion sense are important to her. Susan is always smiling, always happy, and she looks directly at you with her bright and cheery eyes when you speak with her; you always know she's listening.

"I really don't know what to say . . . I . . . I just . . . my memory isn't always so good!" Susan laughed nervously.

I tried to make her feel at ease. After all, few of us feel comfortable when there's a tape recorder running. So I eased her into the conversation, saying, "I'm sure you can remember enough of the times I was staying over the weekend with you guys. Me and Kristina, our little dance parties. I mean, I think of the little things I remember when she and I were little and we'd do little performances on Grandpa and Grandma's fireplace."

"Well," Susan responded, "you were at our house a lot, you know, because my daughter was an only child, and you were as well, so you were always over at our house, and you always played so well together. There weren't a lot of eventful things, you know, you got along so well, and you were just always together. The Brewster story is always the story that sticks out in my mind. When we got our Jack Russell terrier, I had him shipped up from California as a puppy. We all went to the airport to pick him up because he was shipped air cargo. So we went to Alaska Air Freight to pick him up, and of course, we waited and waited because it takes a good time for them to come to cargo claim once the plane comes in. We waited, and we were so excited to get this puppy that was supposed to be my daughter Kristina's birthday present. And we waited, and of course, there he was, and he was just cute and cute cute!"

I responded, "Oh god, he was sooo cute!"

Susan continued, "Yeah, he was so cute! And he was so excited. And he was everything we'd hoped he would be. And . . . I get emotional . . . that . . . now he's gone . . ."

I could hear her choking back tears, and I waited for her to continue.

"And then he barfed in the car!" she said, with a release of laughter.

"Yeah, he was a little nervous about that ride!" I said, encouraging her to go on.

"Yeah, he barfed in the car. Anyway," said Susan, "that was like one of our most exciting things, I think, that we really did with Brewster. We were very excited—and did we take him to the billiard room?"

"Oh yeah!" I affirmed.

Susan continued, "Probably, because we were on our way to the poolroom. We had a billiard room, which my ex-husband and I had, and that was up in Renton, and you spent a lot of time there with Kristina—a lot of time there. Because that was in between our house and your house. So we'd always—if we'd run and get you, you know, to spend time with Kristina . . . because we 'lived' there, it was open 24-7. We started off with it being open 24-7, and then we slowly just closed the hours a little bit to where it wasn't open 24-7. So Kristina needed company, and you didn't have a lot to do, so we'd go get you, and you'd come over. Yeah, I think we took Brewster up to the billiard room then. You and Kristina would work at the billiard room. Kristina was very sharp, and so were you. And you would work the till, and we would give you both money every day, and you'd go to the dollar store."

I paused to reminisce. "Bartells and the dollar store, ah yes," I said.

"Bartells and the dollar store," Susan repeated. "And then you'd go get pizza?"

"Yeah," I said, "and we'd go to the bowling alley next door too."

"What was at the bowling alley that you did?" Susan inquired.

"We would just bowl sometimes and kind of hang out," I recalled.

"We had an arcade in our billiard room," said Susan. "And the arcade, you know, there was pinballs, you know, and video games, just video games. And you'd play constantly. You know, it sounds like it's not a very good atmosphere for a child, but actually, it was probably fun because it was like toys all day long."

Fond memories of my youth came rushing at me. "We worked 'business,' we felt, because we got to run the till."

I could "hear" Susan smile, as she said, "You'd do the till, and you'd pass out the chips, because, you know, we had candy and chips behind the counter, and you would do that, and it relates to growing up. It all relates to growing up with Grandma and Grandpa, because they would play 'store' for you and Kristina, and they would play 'cash register' all the time. So this was right up your alley, Maria, because you wanted to play 'cash register,' and now you were playing 'cash register' in real life. You loved that.

"Grandpa and Grandma always had 'the agenda' and 'the budget,'" Susan continued. "Your grandpa always had the 'twenty-dollar thing.' For all the kids growing up, he always had the 'twenty-dollar thing,' and that was on 'the agenda.' Whenever they came down to Las Vegas, they had 'the twenty-dollar thing.' So when you went to Las Vegas, they had twenty dollars for you, and Grandpa would take you for the 'twenty-dollar thing.' Sometimes they'd give you a dollar to spend when you were out someplace. Back in the early '80s, twenty dollars went a ways. It doesn't anymore, but it did back then. So all the kids always said, you know, 'Hey, Grandpa, let's do the "twenty-dollar thing."' That was a big deal. It was always the 'twenty-dollar thing.' That was the big 'joke' with Grandpa. Yeah. Your grandpa and you all enjoyed that a lot."

Susan paused again, and said reflectively, "But no, you had a good time at the poolroom, and at poolroom was, that was a lot of years there, we probably—well, let's see, we got the poolroom in, '89 through '95? So there was a good six years there. But you moved to Salt Lake City, and I'm not sure what year you moved, what year you were there. But then Kristina always had all her birthday parties, and you always came to all her birthday parties with all of Kristina's friends, and you knew all her friends. You were always included in all that. But yeah, I don't know when you moved to Salt Lake City . . . that's when you were a teenager, so I'm not sure when that was."

Another pause to reflect, and Susan continued, "But you two got along really well, and you really liked each other. You were really close, and you got along really good—even though there was three years' age difference, you got along very well. Kristina was born in '82, and you were born in '79, but you got along great. You did great. You did real well together. Oh gosh! I just remember that you were real easy to be around! You always seemed to be around us, you know? You enjoyed our company a lot and being around us. It just seemed like it was just a real easy fit. It seemed like you just always enjoyed being with us, and it was just easy, and we always got along really great, and things just worked out really well. You were always a really good student, and you did really well at school . . . so . . . um . . ."

I could tell she was searching for what to say next, and I waited.

Susan went on, "I remember when your mom was married to Mike, it seemed like then you kind of had a family there, you know, and things were working out. But it kinda wasn't. I don't remember too much about your situation, you know? Your mom and I weren't real close, so . . . um, you know I wasn't really around in that situation. And then it seemed like then they broke up, so that didn't pan out. And I kinda heard later that he wasn't real nice to you, but then I thought he was. So I don't know. I don't really know your situation and how *that* was. You know, it kind of looked like it was going to be an ideal fit, but then I don't know what happened with that . . .

"And then you left for Salt Lake City, and we didn't see you for a few years, so when you came back, you were a teenager, and then we didn't spend a lot of time together. You were kind of—you know how teenagers are—you were out of high school, and you went to the University of Washington, and we didn't see you much. Kristina was still in high school, so I spent more time with you in that poolroom time. That was kind of in your younger years. Once you got out of high school and came back from Salt Lake City, we didn't really spend a lot of time together.

"We saw you, of course, if we had family things, and we got together, and then things were always just like they had been. You and Kristina just always got along, and that was just as it used to be. You know how kids are—girls get boy-crazy. My daughter was the same way! She was off doing her own thing. And when you were in college, I didn't see you at all!

"As a matter of fact, before your accident, I don't even think I saw you for a long time. I'd sent you a birthday card in October. You know, it was that time of your life! Kristina had seen you. She went down to Medusa. Kristina had just turned twenty-one when she came there to see you.

"I didn't go to your graduation. You were never that way. You never had birthday parties, you never had graduation parties, you never celebrated anything like that. Your mom was like that. She never had birthday parties for you. You didn't go to graduation from high school in Salt Lake City because they were Mormon, and they didn't really accept you. You didn't like high school at all!

"I went to visit you in Salt Lake. You always had horses, growing up. Your mom had a horse, and I had a horse, and I you kept my horse for a short while. My husband and I ride motorcycles, and we rode on a trip back to see you when you had my horse in Salt Lake. We stopped, and we took you to dinner when your mom was on a trip to Europe or something."

"Oh yeah," I said, "that's right, she was in Germany on a European tour of horse shows and stuff!"

"So we went to that place where you throw everything on the floor?" asked Susan. "Did we go there?"

"Yeah," I said. "The Lone Star, and they'd give you little metal buckets of peanuts."

"Yeah," she said. "We went there, and I'll never forget, your mother had a dead chicken in the freezer because she used to do taxidermy, and she'd pick up dead carcasses along the road. I went to get some ice, since it was hot in the middle of summer in Salt Lake City, and there was this dead carcass wrapped in a big garbage bag."

I laughed. "All clean and ready to put together!"

"Yeah," Susan continued. "And we got to visit my horse, and we gave her some bananas."

"I remember cleaning her stall!" I said.

"She always pooped in one spot!" Susan replied.

"She was good," I said. "I actually remember her, because her little lip would curl up, and she'd get all excited . . ."

"And she'd 'talk,'" said Susan. "We used to go to horse shows together. Didn't you used to go to the horse shows with me? With Joey and Hale?"

"I loved their house, let's just say they made it look fabuloussss!" I quipped.

That made Susan laugh. "How old were you when you moved to Salt Lake?"

"Fifteen," I replied.

"So you hung out at the poolroom until about that time?" Susan inquired.

"Yes," I said. "So it wasn't much of a surprise later when my first bartending job was at Belltown Billiards, and what's funny about that is that my uncle Richard was the man who recovered all the pool tables at Belltown Billiards too!"

"Yeah," Susan said, "and you knew a little about playing pool then too! Did you ever whip 'em?"

"Well," I responded, "I was usually working, and I'd watch. I was cocktailing—which meant I was down around the pool tables—some people, the way they played, well, I'd think, 'They could have done that better!'"

"You know, stuff like that!" Susan laughed. "Yeah, absolutely! And then, when did you move back to Seattle?"

"In '98," I replied, "after I'd graduated early from high school. I started to go to college for a little bit, and I was a nursing assistant, and it was that summer."

"Because then you had your little rollover accident, driving back home from Salt Lake," said Susan.

"Yeah," I replied. "Yeah, and Grandpa was there! Boom, boom!"

"Grandpa drove right over, didn't he?" said Susan.

"Yep!" I replied. "To Idaho in the Cadillac!"

"I remember I was working in the Admiral Club for American Airlines," Susan said. "And I got the phone call that you'd had an accident, and that was like, 'Oh my gosh!'"

"That was my first car," I said. "It was a '95 Toyota Tercel two door, and I was leasing it, and I was making the payments on it every month."

"I imagine it was a little flat after that," said Susan. "The roof was a little flat . . ."

"It was totaled," I said, "but none of my Fiesta Ware dishes that were in the trunk were broke, so it was good!"

"Packaged well!" Susan complimented.

"Hey!" I said. "I still have 'em! You know?"

"And then you moved right back to the cabin on Lake Kathleen." Susan recalled. "And you had to work for a year because you had to get your residence before you went back to the University of Washington."

"Right," I confirmed. "Otherwise, they'd charge you three times the amount, and I was like, 'Screw that. I'm not paying that!' So that's when I worked at Nordstrom's, and oh, the cross-dressers at Nordstrom!"

"Well," Susan replied. "Okay, now I used to see you at Nordstrom's, and I was thinking I didn't see you much when you went back to school, but I did see you at Nordstrom's. We'd come and visit you."

"Of course you did," I confirmed. "And Uncle Steve would do these joke calls. I started in hosiery, and that's where I saw cross-dressers for the first time, and I learned, 'We don't do control top! It's too tight there!' But when I worked in handbags—and let me go on about handbags—if you carry what you call a purse, you bought it at Kmart, okay? You don't call a handbag a purse. Anyway, Uncle Steve started doing these joke calls when I was working in handbags, and he'd go, 'I'm looking for a purse for my wife,' and he knew that would get me!"

"You'd say, 'We do not have purses here, we only have handbags!'" Susan said, laughing.

"Yep! Yeah!" I said, laughing along with her.

"Yeah," Susan continued. "I remember we'd come and visit you there. Yeah, we called Nordstrom the Mother Ship."

"And we'd go to the Rack together," I said, "because I'd still get my discount, and we'd go, 'Woo-hoo!' I was so excited!"

"How long did you work there?" asked Susan. "The whole time you were in college?"

"No," I replied. "I was probably there for about a year, because when I started college, I did a couple of internships to get credits, and doing both just wasn't working. Then all of a sudden, I was twenty-one, and oh, I can work at a bar, and there's this cash thing. Hello! That was great!"

"I don't think I saw you too much after that," Susan said reflectively. "You were working nights and going to school during the day."

"And during the day, it was study or nap," I said. "That was about it!"

"You came to visit when we lived in our condo." Susan recalled. "And Grandma and Grandpa came to visit, and you were wearing those leopard pants!"

"Yes, I was," I responded, very quietly.

"They were cute, though!" Susan said cheerily. "They were very cute on you!"

"It's good that I was small enough to wear those, because if I was big . . ." I said, shaking my head.

"You would have been a big leopard!" Susan quipped, and we both laughed. "I was going to say something," Susan continued, "and then I lost my train of thought. I'm sure it'll come to me here. Oh! We were talking about graduation! You finished college right before your birthday, so you actually would have graduated with Kristina's class of '04, right?"

"Right," I confirmed, "because they only do graduation at the end of every spring quarter."

"Because we were talking about that when Kristina graduated," said Susan.

"I know my name was on the graduation class list," I said, "but I wasn't there because I was just out of the hospital."

"Did you get your diploma? Do you have it?" Susan inquired.

"No, I don't," I responded. "I don't think I have it."

"You should have that!" Susan stated sternly. "You worked darn hard for that, you know? And your degree was in communications?"

"Well," I replied, "speech communications specifically, but then they merged the two fields of speech communications and communications together and just called them communications. That was right before I graduated. Kristina's turned twenty-one about six months before my accident. She came in to visit me at Belltown Billiards when I was bartending, but see, that's about when my memory stops from the accident."

Susan paused and drew a deep breath, and then said, "I got the call at one-something in the morning from Lizzy, and you know, it was one of those calls when you got the call, you just went, 'Oh, okay,' and you don't really realize how serious it is. I was just thinking okay, and I put the phone back down, and I lay back down and didn't really realize how serious it was. And then it was like, 'Oh! I have to go to the hospital!' I called her right back and said for her to drive over to my house, and then I'll drive. So I was frantically getting ready, and she was at my house fast from Tacoma. They were talking to Mom on the way, and Mom was saying that she didn't think you were going to make it."

"Were Grandpa and Grandma getting on the plane at that point?" I asked.

"No," said Susan. "We were all talking on the phone, and no one really knew what had happened. It was just some wood or something about wood. I called Kristina, and I told her, so she was coming to the hospital. It was when we were at about the Kent-Desmoines exit that Mom said she didn't think you were going to make it, and we said that we were just driving, we're just going there, and we were just focused.

"Of course, there was no traffic on the road, and we made it there really quick. We drove right to Harborview, parked the car as fast as we could, and we went to emergency, and they kind of pushed us into a little room to the side where everyone was already gathered because they lived so much closer. Everyone was just so tearful, and we all hugged each other, and all we could do was just sit there, waiting.

"Bobby was in the room with you. He was the only one that had gone in there to see you. He was the only one that had looked. For the rest of us, it was just a waiting game in that room. We waited there for a while, and then they took us upstairs. We saw you on the way, but I don't know if you were covered, we saw you, but I don't know if you were covered up—"

"That's what I've been told," I interjected, "that I was covered up because even the staff had a hard time dealing with it."

"You were covered up," Susan continued. "As far as I know, none of us saw you but Bobby, but I'm trying to think if we went in there and saw you covered up. I think so . . . it's just . . . I remember we were sent to the room on the side. It took two hours for organ donation. All the questions they asked—"

"It says it on my driver's license, they should just take 'em!" I said.

"No . . ." Susan said cautiously, "No, it wasn't that. It's all the questions they want to know. They want to know about every sexual partner. They want to know about every question about everything! It's very detailed. It's not just 'Here's your organs,' it's an inch thick of forms on organ donation, and I couldn't believe that. It was a two-hour ordeal, and it just went on and on."

"So everyone's around," she continued. "And there's chaplains and counselors. It was just something else, something that you never ever want to go through, because you're told this person's gone. And basically, we thought you were gone, and we went through the whole process of it, and everyone's sobbing and grieving and going through this process. I know that you were covered, and I think we all went and said good-bye to you. Then we left. It was probably five in the morning, five thirty, six in the morning. By that time,

Mom and Dad had made arrangements and were en route from Las Vegas. I had called work, and they were helping to arrange to meet them coming in. We went to the house, I went home, and Lizzy went home from there. Mom and Dad arrived, you know—time frame, I have no idea what time frame. The whole day was just a blur. I know I went and picked them up at the airport and brought them to the house. At this point, they thought you were gone too. It wasn't until we went to Bobby's that we found out you had moved your hand, and we took the ferry right over, went from Port Orchard to Bremerton and got on the ferry, and went right to the hospital, of course.

"I had been up all night. We'd all been up all night, which didn't matter, you know. We were all just strung out on adrenaline. We came to the hospital, and from there on out, we just camped at the hospital. I ended up getting a week off, and I was there every day all day long for that week. When I did go do my shift, I did my four-hour shift because I was part time, and I would just ride the bus from the airport every day after work and stay all day and then go home, and go to work, and come back again. I think we did that for the two months you were at Harborview.

"That first week was the bad week. It was the worst week. Until they did those surgeries on you to rebuild . . . After they did those surgeries, to see you was just incredible. Your face, your head was just the size an extremely large pumpkin.

"I've heard I kind of had 'alien head,'" I said.

"Well, it was horrible!" Susan replied. "I don't mean just looking, I mean it was just the size, the swelling, the staples. The staples went on forever. I don't know how many staples they had in you, but it was just unreal. Before they did the surgery, the rotting of the flesh, there were just two days of rotting flesh. I remember asking the nurse, 'What is that smell?' And she said it was just the rotting flesh before they did that surgery. It was just horrendous. It was like, don't they need to do it now? Because it happened on a Sunday night, and they didn't do the surgery until Thursday or Friday, and you could just smell the rotting flesh! But the nurses were fabulous. You had the best ER nurses, you know, trauma nurses that you couldn't even imagine. And you had a lot of friends camping out that first week."

"I know my friend Troy was there . . ." I said, trailing off as I tried to recall more of whom I was told was there.

"I cried a lot," Susan replied. "Of course, we all did, but it was like, 'Okay, straighten up!' We just had to go through it. We had to be there and just go through it. It was a long process. Every day you just got better—watching you go from that huge bigness, you know, the swelling, and to watch it go down, and things got better, and then the staples go.

"There were a lot of frustrations at the hospital too. [ ] board, 'She's blind!' But they'd come in and say things t[ ] things, and it was like, 'Read the board! Read the board!' [ ] because it was like, 'Don't you read the charts when you c[ ] like just living in the room, and think, 'Know what's going [ ] frustrated! It would just drive us nuts!"

"I like being told about the language I would use," I said. "The F-word was the thing!"

"A lot of F-words," Susan replied. "Yeah, and you'd tell Grandma a lot of things that she didn't need to know." She laughed. "You didn't want to be in the room alone, so someone always felt like they had to stay with you. The hospital didn't want to put a person in the room with you, so our goal was to always have someone with you because you'd try to get up, but you'd lose your equilibrium. We were afraid you'd fall, and we didn't want you to fall on your head. Your head had a ton of staples. You didn't know where you were, and you were confused, so we wanted someone to be with you at all times.

"We had a really hard time with the hospital. We wanted the hospital to give you a caregiver at all times. That was a constant battle. Every time we thought we had it worked out, they would move you to a different floor, and then we'd have to go through it all over again.

"Then you were moved to Good Samaritan, and I rode with you in the quote, unquote 'ambulance,'" Susan said, making air quotes with her fingers. "It was really just a van that they provided to get you to Good Sam. I was appalled and had to give them a call when we got there. Thank goodness that you are blind and could not see it, because it was filthy, filthy dirty, and there were things rolling all over the place, and I just thought, you know, 'Really?' It was a medical transport van, and it was another typical deal in the care. Some of it was excellent, and then you'd get a bad deal.

"You had motion sickness really bad." Susan recalled. "And we had a barf bag for you, and there really wasn't a place for you to sit in the back of the vehicle. It didn't really have seats, and we had to makeshift a seat for you. And it was dirty, and I was just grossed out. I just was so mortified, and I called and I just really gave them—in a nice way—the riot act. It was just so appalled by them showing up with a van in that condition. It was just so degrading. To provide transportation without seats and seat belts is just ridiculous! I would have refused it, but we had waited and waited. Trying to get discharged from a hospital is such a prolonged event anyway, and it was just one more deal.

"They didn't want to discharge you because they wanted you to go to rehab there. We had to fight to get you into Good Samaritan. It took three hours to get you discharged, and then the van took a while to get there. So en the van showed up, it was like, 'Let's just get going!' Good Sam was waiting for us.

"Lizzy and I had gone down and looked over the facility, and we interviewed people there, and we were really feeling good about it. We felt that we had made the right choice. So we were anxious to get you there and get you on the right track. The rehab that had you doing at Harborview was just mundane tasks, things that you knew, and it wasn't helping you make any progress. And we just wanted to get you going. So we got you to Good Sam—not in a very dignified way, though!

"When we got you to Good Sam, you called us a lot in the middle of the night, do you remember that?" Susan asked.

I smiled and said, "I remember when I first got a phone back in my hand, I was ready to dial!"

"Yeah, you were," Susan confirmed. "But in the middle of the night, you'd call and you'd cry and say, 'I'm lonely! I want to get out of here!' So Lizzy and I would come at one in the morning, and we'd sit by your bed. Some people said we shouldn't do that, that you'd just call all the time, but we felt bad, and we knew the condition you were in, and we felt it was the right thing to do."

"I remember you and Richard would both be there." I recalled. "And I'd be doing the physical therapy thing."

"What's funny about that," said Susan, "is the occupational therapist turned out to be my neighbor from my condo that I used to live in! Small world! She was a sweetheart too."

"I remember a lot when you were there," I continued. "I remember Bobby there and Liz. I remember being walked around by nurses all the time and going to the bathroom all the time . . ."

"Oh, that was the thing!" said Susan. "You always felt like you had to go to the bathroom, and I don't know what it was, if it was the medication, I don't know if it was your feeding tube. I just don't know what it was. As soon as we'd take you and put you in your bed, you'd say, 'I've gotta go to the bathroom,' and it was constant. I mean, annoying constant, and I'm sure it was annoying for you! But it was just constant. Constant. So that was why we wanted to have a caregiver with you all the time, because you were up and down, and we were afraid you'd fall. You were unsteady, and you couldn't get around, of course, because you weren't seeing. I'd forgotten about the bathroom thing. Oh, it was constant! The bathroom thing just didn't go away."

"See, I don't remember Harborview at all," I said. "I remember parts, maybe the last couple of weeks at Good Samaritan. I remember going to what they called classes, where I would meet with different occupational therapists . . ."

"You were annoyed," said Susan. "You were totally annoyed with that."

"I was irritated," I recalled. "They'd read me little snippets of stories and ask me to repeat them, and pure crap came out of my mouth even though it was all in here in my brain, but it just wasn't coming out the way I heard it. It was in there, and I could think of it, but I just couldn't say it."

"Do you remember the pool players coming to see you at Good Sam?" Susan asked.

"No, I don't," I replied.

"Well, you were on a lot of drugs," Susan reflected. "Thorotin for nerve-ending damage, which was strong. You were on a lot of antipsychotics and a lot of things because of your brain injury. They didn't know what to do. They just didn't know what to do. But Richard, my ex, had a pool benefit for you . . ."

"Oh yeah." I recalled. "I've run into some of those different guys that were in it and did stuff with it or went to it just since I moved to West Seattle."

Susan continued, "Real top players from across the United States that were legends twenty years ago and on TV then. You don't see them on TV anymore, but really class-act guys came in. They went to the hospital and met you, and then they did the benefit at Kennedy High School in Burien. They raised about twelve or thirteen thousand dollars for you, which was really nice of them. And they all signed a pool table, and Kristina's boss ended up buying it. And Kristina's friend Desiree's parents did all the photography and donated all that."

"I remember after I came home," I said, "and my first time staying at your place. I remember that your dog, Brewster, was there, and I remember this and that. I remember sleeping on the daybed, and he jumped right in and went right to my tummy. I slept on my side, and he went right to his little snuggle spot and curled right up, and I was like, 'Awww . . .'"

"I still have a little mark on my daybed mattress cover where your feeding tube leaked," laughed Susan.

"It was a leaker!" I confirmed, laughing along with her. "I remember being at Big Lots or something like that with my friend Misty. We were walking around, and all of a sudden, it was like, *wooshhhh!* 'Clean up on aisle four!'"

"You had that feeding tube for a long time," Susan said, her voice trailing off empathetically.

"I remember getting it out hurt," I recounted. "I went back for surgery to get my braces off, and then they took the feeding tube out. I remember they didn't take the feeding tube out until the anesthesia wore off and I was awake. Somebody's hand holding the skin down around the tube, and there was a hand attempting to pull the tube out. I was screaming at the top of my lungs because it hurt so bad, so they had a doctor come in and give me little shots of Novocaine all around it."

"They should have done that at the beginning of the surgery!" Susan said insistently. "It had to be in there pretty deep, plus had been in there for four months!"

"It was the same thing later too," I continued, "where I had facial surgeries, and they had little tubes coming out that were collecting excess fluids and blood. Trying to pull that out was like, 'Owwww! Seriously? Ugh!'"

Susan paused again, and then said, "I remember when you first spoke. No one knew if you were going to talk, and I remember you were down in that one wing that you didn't like very well. Didn't you say *Coca-Cola* first? I was there, I remember you wanted a Coke. You were thirsty, and I think you wanted a Coke. You know, sometimes you just want a thing, and I think that's what you wanted. I think you said that. We were just so excited. You could have just sworn like a truck driver, and I would have been happy! We just wanted to hear you talk, and boy, we were just so excited when you talked.

"You had that tracheal tube," Susan continued, "and for so long you couldn't talk. As soon as they took that out we were all just waiting, and oh, how we had waited for that! They kept saying they were going to take the trache out this date, and then they were going to take it out this date, and they were going to take it out then. You know, waiting for the doctors to come at Harborview was just a case of you never know when. But I think you said *Coke* first. It was like waiting for your baby's first words!

"And then we couldn't get you to shut up after that!" Susan said teasingly, making me smile, and we both laughed.

"My friend Hale came to visit you," she continued, "and he brought you this obnoxious stuffed thing that swore. You'd slap it down, and it had a noise, and I said, 'Don't give her that!' It said something like 'Goddamn it!' or 'Shit!' or something like that, and I said, 'Why are you giving her that?' He thought you'd think it was funny. I ended up taking it home because I didn't want to leave it there. Your little cousin Kate would come to visit you. That was when you looked pretty good. By that time your face wasn't as swollen, so Lizzy had brought her kids, and Kate was only like three years old, and she didn't want to bring her earlier. So I thought, 'I'm not going to have that around with Kate,' but Hale just thought it was the funniest thing in the world! He got such a kick out of that!

"You know." Susan recalled. "I have some things stored under the house that some kids in elementary school did for you, and I need to see if I still have them. All kinds of hand-drawn get-well cards and stuff. I'll have to look and see what I have, how many mementos I saved. I saved a whole lot of articles and things. I have a whole packet of articles and some video tapes. I've saved almost all the newspaper articles."

"So let me ask you," I said, smiling. "What was it like the first time you took me shopping? I do remember going to the mall or something."

Susan pondered for a moment, and then said, "Well, the first time we took you shopping, it was kind of funny, because you had your prosthetic eyes in, and we went out to lunch, and people kept looking at you, and they had no idea you were blind. They were looking at you, and you were 'looking' right back at them. You were 'staring' at them, and they had no idea! It was pretty funny!"

I laughed, and said, "I remember we went to Bahama Breeze, and we were sitting in a booth. Now you know, I turn my face toward voices. So Liz would be talking, and then she'd say, 'Quit staring at me!'"

We both had a hearty laugh. When we'd caught our breath, Susan said, "And now you're bartending again! I suppose you can do that because of free pouring."

"That, and the gun," I replied. "You hold it down for whatever, and it happens. I can't tell you what's what unless I have the gun in my hand, and even then, I just do it."

"I know. It's all rhythm," Susan said knowingly.

"And on that television interview I did." I laughed. "I wasn't focused on what I was doing, so I missed the glass!"

"Did you spray the reporter?" Susan inquired.

"Yep," I confirmed jokingly. "Gave 'em a little spritz! Yes, I did! No, not really."

And we laughed.

JIM STEVENS

Jim Stevens is a paramedic and works for King County Medic One, considered a world leader in emergency medical services. Medic One's paramedics are trained by a joint program of the University of Washington, Harborview Medical Center, and the Seattle Fire Department. Jim was the first medically trained individual to arrive on the scene of my accident, and without his skills and experience, I wouldn't be alive today. In order to better understand what happened to me during the most critical hours of my life and how I survived, I sat down to talk with Jim about his recollections and how what happened to me affected his life.

"Are you up for this?" asked Jim.

"Sure," I replied. "I don't remember that night, so I don't care."

"It was fairly late," Jim began. "It had been busy night for Medic One Unit Five. Medic Five is one of our busier trucks for South King County Medic One. South King County is a little bit unique in that we only do advanced life support. We don't do any fire suppression. If you see a South King County Medic One truck at a fire, it's because we're there to be available to the firemen if they have issues while they're fighting the fire. We don't pull hose. We do get issued bunker gear, but I think I've put mine on twice in fourteen years of being there. Prior to that, I worked as a firefighter.

"That night," Jim continued, "Steve Perry and I were working Medic Five. It was after nine at night, which is when we change positions on the truck. For the first half of the shift, which starts at nine in the morning, Steve was 'in charge'—quote, unquote—then I'm 'in charge' for the next twelve hours. And so that means I was riding in the officer's seat. The officer rides in the passenger seat, and the other guy drives. Steve Perry was in charge of doing the IV skills—putting the tube in, starting the IV, and stuff.

"So it was after nine o'clock, and I was in charge, and Steve was doing the driving. We responded to your call. I think it went out after eleven thirty. I think it was real close to midnight. I remember them describing your condition. We got a short report from dispatch, and dispatch was still on the phone with bystanders calling with their cell phones.

"We were on our way to the call. I remember Steve at one point on the drive saying this could be really bad, and I go, 'Yeah, you know?' So we were a little bit fired up about it. We got there, and I remember pulling the gurney out of the back of the truck. Normally when the medics show up, we get there and we evaluate the patient, and we decide whether we're going to transport or not, whether the patient is sick enough, if you will, to be riding with the medics. In this case, from the reports on the radio on the way there, clearly you were going to ride with me."

Jim reached out and took my hand, asking, "I can hold your hand?" I squeezed back, silently affirming that it was okay, so Jim continued, "You were a keeper, as we call them!" I laughed at this and smiled.

Jim continued, "We pulled up to the scene, I jumped out, I grabbed the gurney out of the back of the truck, and I started walking over. We were able to park real close to your vehicle. Somehow, a guardian angel put your vehicle off the main lanes, out of traffic, without hitting the guardrail."

"That's me!" I laughed quietly. "I know how to drive." My Jeep was in the right-hand breakdown lane. I had brought it safely to a stop and even put it into park before losing consciousness.

"I stepped out," said Jim, "and saw a firefighter, and I said to him, 'Let's get her in the back of the truck,' because that's my comfort zone. You get in the back of my truck, and I've got everything I need there. I know where everything is. It's light, whereas everything out there on the side of the road at night in February is too dark, too cold. So we started moving in your direction, and one of the firefighters said we might want to take a look at what we've got first, implying that you were really, really bad."

Jim paused for a moment, concerned about what he was saying, and said, "Sorry."

"It's okay," I replied.

"That particular firefighter, I think, was a lieutenant," Jim continued, "and he had probably been around for twenty years in EMS in Renton, which is not unknown to have some trauma. That's a lot of experience saying, 'Yeah, I'm not sure that we should continue working this direction.'

"I remember taking a look at you, and as I walked up to you, you were lying there next to your Jeep Liberty. And the two firefighters that were working with you trying to help you breathe, one of them is now a medic—Orson Gurney Jr.—which is confusing because his dad was a Renton firefighter too. Orson Gurney was assigned to A12 that night, and he stepped up to me . . ."

Jim trailed off on that recollection, and explained, "We have this thing called a bag-valve mask, and it's basically to put a mask over your nose and mouth, and it has a rubber seal, and then we help you breathe. The problem with you was the only thing left of your face was your lower jaw and your eyebrows. The rest of this, everything in between, was not there, not right, not anatomically correct. So Orson was struggling to find a seal. As he's bagging, the air's just moving out through the blood and tissue, and it's not getting air into your lungs like we needed.

"Orson steps up to me and says, 'I don't know if we're doing her any good, Jim.' And he just had this look of . . . Orson doesn't like to fail at anything. None of us do. And he had this look, like, 'I'm struggling, and I can't get it done!' It's not despair, but it's a lot like that.

"You were still trying to breathe, and I remember thinking, 'She's still trying to breathe, so we're going to keep going here. We're gonna keep helping.' So *click-click*, you were in the back of the truck. I remember looking on your hand for an IV point on your hand. When people lose blood at a significant rate, their body, something about their nervous system, says, 'My blood pressure's getting low. I'm going to increase my heart rate, and I'm gonna start shutting down my periphery.' It's a defense mechanism, and when you do that, you lose the blood in the veins in your hands. So we started a central line, which is a subclavian IV right by your neck, underneath your clavicle. While I was doing that, Steve went ahead and did the intubation, which required moving some tissue out of the way."

I laughed.

"Sorry," Jim said, concerned that I might be uncomfortable with the graphic nature of his description. "You're sure you're good with this?"

"It sounds funny to me!" I said, laughing even louder. It just sounds so weird to me, because again, I have no recollection of anything after the accident, and that they had to do this sounded like it was happening to someone else. It's just so weird to think that it was me this happened to.

Reassured, Jim continued, saying, "At the time, we were serious pucker-factor. The two firefighters and Steve were able to get the endotracheal tube in. That usually requires finding the tongue, which was easier for you because there was nothing there. There was no nose. There was no upper jaw. There was nothing there to block the view of your tongue. So once the tissue was moved out of the way, we used a laryngoscope blade. We used the curved blade instead of the straight blade. A *blade* is a maybe a bad word for it, since it's a piece of metal that we use to sweep the tongue out of the way to look for the vocal cords. Normally, there's the bridge of the nose and everything else that you look over the top to see the vocal cords. None of that was there. So it was slide the tongue, there's the cords, put the tube in, away we go.

"My IV went about that smoothly as well. Subclavian IVs go in pretty quick. There's a huge vessel right underneath your clavicle, and it's a straight shot in, and it's a big line, so we can move a lot of fluid through it. Then it was just a matter of securing you to the backboard, a C-collar because you had taken a serious hit to the head and neck, and we weren't sure if there was any C-spine injury. So collared and boarded, completely stripped so we can see any other injuries—you know, you can't treat what you can't see—so we strip everybody."

This still sounds weird to me, and I can't picture it in any way. How can your face be like that, like it was open like some book or something? It makes me think there are hinges in your face or something that it can open up that way. Of course I'm not stupid, and I know it doesn't work like that, but it sounds so strange. And why wouldn't it? It's not an everyday experience.

Jim continued, saying, "IV'd, intubated, we turned around on the freeway. You were between Northeast Thirtieth and Sunset on 405, so we drove to Sunset and did a loop and headed back on 405 across the I-90 bridge and on over to Harborview.

"Medics aren't assigned to every call here in King County. We have a tiered system, which is really unique. The rest of the world does it different. The rest of the world puts a paramedic on every truck, and they oversaturate their systems with too many paramedics. So when they do get there, they're not as . . . they're not . . . they haven't seen as many sick people, say, as Steve and I do. And so their skills aren't maybe as sharp as ours, and a lot of systems don't allow for that central-line placement. So they would have kept struggling, struggling, struggling to get an IV. We probably would have gotten you intubated without the IV, but some systems don't allow for the central-line placement, which allowed me to give some paralyzing medicine so that your vocal cords didn't slap shut every time they're touched with the endotracheal tube. So it's a system that we are very proud of here in King County that allows me to paralyze patients and just get the work that needs to be done done and take care of folks that need it, like you did. From the time of the tone-out to the time we pulled on ramp at Harborview was just twenty-eight minutes. So all that got done and the transport in a half hour.

"Do you know what Kerlix cling is?" Jim said, easing back on to what happened. "We have lots of different things to hold bandages, and it's something that holds the bandage. They're sterile, but they're not designed to go right on top of your 'owie.' Once we got the endotracheal tube in, we're kind of standing there, and you have to hold that, you have to secure that to somebody's head so that it doesn't come out, because if it comes out, it could dislodge and go into your stomach, and then you're bagging their stomach full of air and not their lungs—and they could die that way. Dislodgement of an endotracheal tube is a cardinal sin.

"For you," Jim continued, "the endotracheal tube holders we have rest on your lips. It rests on your teeth, upper and lower, and it's a great big . . . it kind of looks like a football mouthpiece, and the tube comes out through it, and we have a screw on that that holds the tube right there. But there was nothing there to secure it. There was no 'structure' to hold that tube, so we used Kerlix, which come in rolls, one this way and two that way, and the tube came out through the middle of that, and we secured the tube to that. We padded that area so that it would suck down the padding. Then there's that piece, and the cord around the neck that goes up through and loops back through and you can secure it, so that as they move their head, they can't pull the tube out.

"Not that you were moving," said Jim. "We took care of that and made sure that you were comfortable and unconscious.

"I remember them undoing all that at Harborview, and there was a rupture of your artery that fed your left optic nerve. I remember when they took that bandage off, there was a geyser of blood. And they were trying to stop all these little bleeders . . .

"The problem with the face and the neck and the upper chest region is that it blushes, so any injury to a blushing area is a profuse bleeder. Any injury to a zone that will blush is a profuse bleeder.

"That's pretty much all I remember from the night of your accident. The part about you, that is. As for me and Steve, I remember afterwards, we went back to the station. We wrote the report. I wrote a very detailed report that particular night. I try and write a lawyer-proof report on all my calls, but I remember taking extreme caution in having lots of detail on this one.

"Then I remember going back to the station of Medic Five that night. Sometimes we're housed by ourselves, and sometimes we share quarters with a fire station. In that particular era of Medic Five, we were sharing at Station 14, south of 405 on Lind Avenue, just north of IKEA. We were there, and I remember coming back to the station. It was about two in the morning, and I remember just being in a daze, just like, 'What just happened?' It was clearly obvious that this was a gorgeous young girl, and it was just like, 'What just happened?' And you know, processing that . . .

"Steve said, 'I think I need to just watch some TV and just kind of get something else in my head so that I can go fall asleep, otherwise, I'll just lie there and replay that call in my head, over and over and over.' So we did. We watched TV until we both fell asleep around the TV, and then we straggled off to bed.

"I called Harborview the next morning—gosh, I don't know what time, probably around ten o'clock—and got a hold of Dr. Kopas, who . . ."

Jim trailed off again in thought, and then asked, "Had you ever been to Harborview prior to your incident?"

"I don't believe so," I responded.

Jim resumed, describing it in terms of his experience. "There's an area in there, a little room with a bunch of windows in it, and we call it the fishbowl. It's where Dr. Kopas . . . if you have an ass-chewing coming from Dr. Kopas, he'll take you into the fishbowl so nobody can hear what's going on, but they can see him chewing your ass.

"Every morning, Kopas—at that time he was in charge of the emergency room—and all the young doctors were practicing in there, and they'd go in there and they'd have a month of—it's just like hell month. They'd learn a lot, but every morning, he'd go in there and review all the medical incident report forms, or MIRFs, from the night before and chew ass on whoever needed it in the fishbowl.

"I called Harborview just to check up on you and see what your status was because I wasn't sure, and of course, it was on the news, and they were talking about how you were in critical condition. He told me, and I quote, 'Oh, Jimmy, she's dead. Those people die.'"

"Well," I said, "they had sent my mom home with a 'burial package.'"

Jim paused again, then confirmed, "They had sent your mom home with the organ-donation paperwork filled out, and so I kind of swallowed hard and said, 'Damn it.' I remembered thinking during the call that we had seen some pictures when we went through paramedic training. You see pictures of horrible things people had done to themselves, and I remembered seeing this one idiot who had tried to commit suicide with a shotgun. The problem is the barrels are too long, and they end up having to tip their heads back in order to reach the trigger, and when they do that, the remove their chin. This guy's face . . . it's a horrible photo. I remembered thinking if that asshole can survive having done that to himself, then this woman, who didn't do anything wrong, by God, she's going to survive this! I remember feeling that way during the call. So when he told me that you wouldn't survive the next morning, I was pretty down and thinking, 'That sucks.'

"During the course of the week I remember thinking, 'She's been upgraded to stable now, or at least something more stable than critical,' and I'm thinking, 'As far as I'm concerned, Dr. Kopas is the Lord Almighty and a very, very, very smart man, and he told me you died!' So all week long, I'm thinking they're just trying to flush this guy out that lost whatever board off of his truck, and they're just trying to get him to come forward by telling the public that you're improving. That's how I took that. Then by Thursday, I'm working with a guy who had a friend in the ICU, one of your nurses. So we called to talk to him, and he told us, 'Oh no, she's doing better!' I finally came in and saw you on Friday—and all week I had thought you were dead.

"They had done the first surgery on you, and they found that all of your skin was intact, and you wouldn't have to have any grafting. The injury kind of came across your face, rolled your skin up underneath. Initially they were just trying to stop the bleeding, and once they finally did that, then they decided to stop, take a breath, and wait a day. When they started doing the surgery to see how much of you was still there, it was like, 'Wow. All of her skin is here. We're not going to need to do any grafting.'

"I saw you Friday, the day after your surgery. I met your mom and your aunts and your uncle and your grandparents. I think at one point during the visits after that, I even met your dad.

"I remember testifying at the trial during your lawsuit. I loved your attorney. I remember we talked a couple of times before the trial. There was no big prep work or anything, that was interesting. I got off work one morning at Medic Four in North Highline, and I came to the courthouse. He brought me in with very little prep, and he was very nice and walked me through, you know, what was your training like and what's your experience, and this and that, and what kind of schedule do you work. And just to be nice to me, he said, 'And didn't you just get off of one of those shifts this morning?' And I was like, 'Yes, I did.'

"I was looking at the defense attorney's table. There wasn't really daggers. The feeling I was getting from them was more like, 'Ugh. This sucks, and we're on the hook, and this really sucks.' I don't think those people were enjoying having to listen to me testify."

"I remember hearing on the news," I said, "or somebody telling me about it. What did you think about the report that they let loose—I guess it came from the defense, and they put it on the news—that bit about 'her blood alcohol read this . . .'"

"'Well, where did they get that?' is what I thought initially," Jim replied angrily. "Is there disclosure that goes on? I don't know where they got it. As much fluid as you got the night of your injury—you got, if I remember right—something along the lines of ten liters of IV fluid plus a whole bunch of blood, like seventeen units of blood!"

Remembering what I had heard, I agreed. "It was coming out faster than they could put it in."

"Absolutely, it was," Jim said, "so I don't know how any of that could have been remotely accurate, and we gave you some medicine too, several kinds, just me on the way to the hospital. Who knows what Harborview gave you. Then I remember the neurologist came in to see you after they had made the decision—horrible. I can't imagine how miserable it would be to go ahead and say yes, that's what my daughter would want, is to be a donor and help others live.

"That decision was made, and the neurologist has to go in and verify that indeed there is no hope left. And he says, 'Why is the patient still on a sedation drip, a propofol drip?' And the nursing staff says well, 'When we turn it off, she reaches up for her face.' And he goes, 'Well, then what are we doing! We've gotta . . . time out! That's higher brain function! That means something! We can't be doing this!'

"That was when they called your family back to the hospital. Your poor family that night. You were reaching for your face. If they turned off the sedation, you would reach up for your face. That was the part of the decision to not have you be an organ donor."

So I said, "That's funny to me, that I was reaching for my face. I was probably trying to check my mascara or something like that!"

Jim laughed heartily. "I think you were in a lot of pain and reaching up to find out why you were in such pain."

After another a long pause, Jim finally said, "I don't know what else to say. That was by far my most memorable call. I've been in EMS since I got home from college in 1991, so twenty years this year in the fire service as a paramedic and in King County for fourteen of those years. I stick my chest out the hardest for you. I'm very proud of how that call went. The skills went well. The progression from the scene to the hospital went well. Everything went well, and it worked out beyond my wildest expectations of your survival. It has worked out."

I asked, "Did you think that it would be that I'd get from the accident to the hospital okay and then progress from not dead to 'She's alive' to 'She's critical'—from that until how I am now? Did you ever think it would be that much?"

"Maybe it was the time I finally came to see you that Friday," said Jim. "I did go see Dr. Kopas again, and he kind of pulled me off to the side and said, 'Let me tell you what happened. We did this, and we did this, and we had the neurology guy looking at her, evaluating her, and the neurologist finally said, 'Why are we on the propofol drip?' And after that transgression then they—well, not transgression, that transition from being an organ donor to being a patient again . . . Dr. Kopas told me the nurses in the unit are just going out of their minds, upset about 'What are we doing with this beautiful girl? Why are we continuing to keep this person alive? She's gonna be blind. She's gonna be deaf.' This is what he told me about you. 'She's not gonna be able to speak. She's not gonna be able to eat. She's not going to be able to take care of herself one bit. She may not even be cognizant. There may be horrific, way-bad brain damage.' And the nurses were telling the doctors, 'What the hell are you doing? Why don't you let nature take its course here?' And he says, 'We're just gonna wait and see what Maria does. We're just gonna let Maria decide for us what happens from here on out.'

"Apparently, you had been stubborn your entire life, according to your family. I suppose that's why somebody graduates on the dean's list with a communications major. You're that stubborn.

"But yeah," Jim continued, "I guess it's good to talk about things like that. Your progress even from when you left Good Samaritan until now is immense and impressive. Then there were those early times when you came to have dinner at Station 12, and you would talk to the guys and not just communicate to the whole table, but you'd address each individual. Somebody would make a comment, and you would turn and address them. That kind of stuff, those kinds of changes have been magnificent and magnificent to see, miraculous to see. So congratulations to you on that!"

Then Jim asked, "Do you remember coming to dinner with my wife and I and going to one of my kids' shows?"

"Yeah," I responded. "Yeah, in Issaquah. We went to a Chinese restaurant."

"Yeah, and you had a bad headache." Jim recalled. "Are you still having those?"

"Once in a while," I said. "Every once in a while, but it might just be because I had a vodka tonic the night before, and I didn't eat dinner. You know, just something stupid."

"But not everyday crushing headaches like you had at that time," Jim inquired.

"No, nothing like that," I agreed.

Jim recalled more details and said, "I remember thinking taking you to see a show would be fun. My son is an aspiring actor, and he was heavily involved in village theater, and he's done some professional work there, and at the time he was Joseph in *Joseph and the Amazing Technicolor Dreamcoat*. So we went to dinner at a Chinese food place, and then we wandered down the street and went to the show. And it's all singing. It's all musical. There's no lines in it. So that was fun. We hoped that it was fun!"

Thinking about going out to dinner and a show made me wonder what happened to my clothes I was wearing on the night of the accident. "How did my poor outfit fare that night?" I asked. "Probably not good."

"Your outfit got cut off of you unceremoniously," Jim said analytically. "I don't remember what it was even."

"I'm sure it was all in black," I said. "That's what I wore when I was bartending."

"It was obvious that you took very good care of yourself," Jim said, in a mix of professional dispassion and yet in a complimentary way. "You were, and are, in phenomenal shape, and we were just like—that added to the agony of it all, the angst of it all."

Of course, I care about my ride as much or more than my clothes, so I had to inquire, "And then my poor Jeep . . ."

"Yeah," said Jim. "I don't know what happened. We spent zero time looking at the Jeep. Somebody reached through the window, the windshield I think, and unlocked the door and held your hand or something . . ."

"Yeah," I responded. "It was the bus driver. An off-duty Metro bus driver."

Jim continued, sounding a bit sad. "I remember feeling bad for him because, boy, what a horrific thing to have to be the first person on the scene."

I care about how this affected people. "Yes," I responded. "He had problems with that for years after, and if he still does, I don't know."

"Nice guy," Jim said sympathetically. "I remember them interviewing him on one show or another."

I know how I would feel if someone I loved went through that or how I would feel too. "I've heard that his wife might be a therapist. If that's so, I hope that would have helped him get through it."

Jim thought for a moment. "There's things you can't unsee. So when you go to bed at night and you close your eyes, and that's all you see—that recurring little video or picture flashing up—that's no good. You have to put up with that for a long time. The way we got around it was we fell asleep in front of the TV. I'm going to get around processing this by just watching something else until my body says enough and shuts down without my brain's permission. That was a long time ago . . . What year was that?"

"That was '04," I responded.

"Wow," said Jim.

"Yeah, I know," I said, thinking about how much time had passed. "It's going on eight years now."

"That's amazing," Jim reflected.

"I know," I responded.

"Your birthday's coming up in a month too!" said Jim.

"I know!" I exclaimed, trying not to sound too excited. "Halloween! Thirty-two! Yep, the big three-two. But it's not like I plan much for my birthday anymore. Halloween? You don't know what the weather's going to be like. Most of the time it's raining. Although my man had a great idea how to scare kids if we get any trick-or-treaters."

"Oh, I'm sure you will in this neighborhood, won't you?" Jim inquired.

I could tell he was still wondering what I was up to, so I gave in and described the plan. "Well, you know, these come out," I said, pointing to my prosthetic eyes.

Jim began to laugh, and I couldn't resist making him laugh more. "And I can put them in my hand!"

"You guys are *horrible!*" Jim exclaimed, laughing with me.

KRYSTEN

Krysten was my first caregiver. The first person I was able to get along with comfortably. Closest to age, similar tastes, a lot in common. Important for such a close relationship where you have to spend a lot of time together, could talk about whatever.

"I could write a whole book about you and fashion," said Krysten.

"Well, we did go shopping a lot, didn't we?" I said. "Hey, did I tell you that I was recognized in Vegas?"

"By people you didn't know?" said Krysten.

"They recognized me because of that news report on Channel 5. Did you see that one? The one where I was bartending again? It went a little bit viral, and even an Italian bartending website had a link to it because it was on MSNBC," I inquired.

"Really!" Krysten responded.

"In a week, there was almost a million hits," I was pleased to say.

"Wow! Woah!" said Krysten.

"Yeah. Yeah!" I said, full of pride.

"That's so cool!" said Krysten.

"I was so happy, I called my dad. I told him he'd appreciate this and he should look it up. And he was," I said.

"Wow!" responded Krysten. "And to think the last time I'd seen you, you'd just had your jaw surgery done. I don't think I've ever seen you open your mouth like that before!" Krysten said happily.

"Yeah, it was right after," I said.

"I'm so glad for you, Maria!" Krysten said. "That you've come so far and that you've found someone that could do that for you."

"It was in Spokane," I replied.

"That was hard, I know," Krysten said reflectively. "That so . . . great. Great."

"That was a nine-hour surgery. Nine hours! And right here? From here to there?" I said, pointing to a small scar a little less than an inch long in front of my left ear. "That tiny little scar? That's all they did."

"Wow. To go through all that work. How was the recovery?" Krysten inquired.

"The only thing I found out was that there's another antibiotic that I'm allergic to! My body shuts down. I get, like, hives and stuff," I responded.

"That's right," replied Krysten. "I just can't believe how time flies. That's the thing of it. I'm just thinking about the time we spent together. Incredible to think about all the opportunities I got to be with you, and we became friends . . . You stayed at my house."

"I remember it all, especially the way from the living room to the bathroom. I learned it," I said.

"I'd sleep in the living room with you. I'm sure sleeping is a little, you know, different now. Or is it still . . ." Krysten stated.

"I still have to wake up and go to the bathroom every now and then, but it's not like it was," I said.

"Yeah, it was kind of a . . ." Krysten said, trailing off. "When I first met you, you went a lot."

I laughed.

"It's not funny," Krysten stated in a friendly but stern way as she laughed with me. "I remember driving in Renton, and I don't know where we were going, to some appointment you had, and it was the second time I'd taken you anywhere. I remember somebody honking behind me, and you didn't feel good—you were nauseous, really nauseous. I was so concerned about the way you were feeling, and I was driving super slow, and I came to this turn to the right, and somebody honked at me. And I got so mad at that person, and I thought, 'If they only knew! There's this person I'm taking care of in my car! Don't you fucking get it?' I wanted to take down their license number. That was intense! I'd never been with somebody that couldn't see, and I got to help you around. Remember that lady who came out and helped us? I don't remember her name."

"I don't either," I said, "but she was the community services for the blind."

"Is that the woman that worked with your dog, Sam?" Krysten inquired.

"That was another woman, later on," I said.

"And is Sam still helpful to you?" Krysten asked.

"Well, most times it's just me and my man," I responded. "If I just go for a walk and I just take him? He'll go right back into service mode. But if it's us, all three, then he's like, 'Doot du du, du du. I'll piss here, and I'll crap there.' You know . . . But now we've got three dogs all together now. Sadie, Sam, and Nick."

"The first time I met you was in the hospital," said Krysten. "And I don't know if you'd remember anything about that."

"Oh god no!" I exclaimed. "I was on so many drugs then!"

"You had a trache tube in," Krysten continued, "and they were doing something to it. I remember you just wanted to touch my hair. It was like, 'It's so soft! I like your hair!' And that was good, because all I wanted was for you to like me! Whatever it takes! Just feel my hair! And you slept!"

"I know," I replied. "I slept a lot! I remember you taking me to the physical therapist all the time."

"The physical therapist?" Krysten inquired. "For your jaw? That was intense, right? Okay, so I got to stick my fingers in your mouth, and they taught me how to do this jaw massage, and it was like not really helpful, but we did it! You were really good about it."

"We tried!" I exclaimed. "It turned out that there was something wrong that couldn't really be fixed by that!"

"I think the thing that we did most was that we went to Nordstrom!" said Krysten.

"I think we did!" I concurred.

"We would go to the Rack, and you could pick up any shoe, and you could totally tell me exactly what it was. You'd say, 'This is a nice patent leather' and so on. And I learned so much about fashion and all the shoes."

"Oh, the shoe aisles," I said. "The glory!"

"Designer jeans . . ." Krysten reflected.

"Oh yeah," I said.

"Yeah, a lot of shopping and a lot of eating out," said Krysten. "So then everybody would be like, 'So what did you do at work today?' We'd go to Nordstrom, and they ate at Jack in the Box, and we went out to eat, and they were like, 'Bummer for you!'

"And then you had a great vocabulary," Krysten continued, "so I got to pick up on words like *scoach* . . . just all of the things you say that I don't even remember now, like *fashion citation*. Everybody knows that about your personality. It's very contagious. And you taught me how to cook! So when you'd come to my house, I remember you telling me, 'So what do your kids like to eat?' and I'd be like, 'Nothing.' So you'd be, like, you'd make up a whole recipe, and you'd ask 'Do you like this?' and 'Do you like this?' and 'Do you like that?' and pretty soon, instead of deep-frying our chicken nuggets, we're like breading them and baking them, and my whole family is sitting down to eat food that you mainly prepared in my kitchen. I have to say, I was a little bit nervous at first!"

"But after you saw me, it was all right!" I reassured her.

"Yeah!" said Krysten. "You'd just do that! And do you remember how you slept on the couch? I mean do you remember *how* you slept on the couch? How I had the warn Bryce?"

"I remember the little dogs sleeping with me all the time," I said.

"But do you remember what you wore to sleep?" asked Krysten. "Probably what you do now . . ."

"I don't know," I said, blushing.

"You didn't wear anything but your panties," said Krysten.

"Oh! Yeah, that sounds about right!" I exclaimed.

"It was like, 'Okay, kids, if you get up'—because you were on my couch—'be sure that Maria knows that you're up!' because she might just wake up not knowing you're up, and my son Bryce would get a—"

"What's that?" I interjected, laughing.

"Yeah," said Krysten. "That was fun."

"We did a lot of driving," Krysten continued, changing the subject, "and we did a lot of shopping. A lot of eye appointments! That was amazing how many eye appointments. How detailed those people are! Do you still see Rita? Rita taught me how to knit!"

"Yeah, she did! That's right!" I said. "The European knitting style, that's right!"

"She did. And I really miss her too," said Krysten. "She's a neat lady."

"She loves it now," I said. "Because when I go to see her, my man always has jokes for her. She laughs!"

"That's good," replied Krysten. "She's got a great sense of humor, and she's a really neat lady. She's a little fireball!"

"She's a lot like Dr. Ruth, isn't she?" I stated.

"What else would we do?" Krysten said. "You didn't feel good a lot when I first met you. I can tell you feel so much better! I felt so bad, and it was really hard. When I was with you, I really . . . I felt like I just had to watch everything. I felt like I really had to watch out for you."

"Well," I said. "I remember when I would stay at your house, and we would walk to that little park close to your house. That kind of stuff is when I felt better."

"Yeah, we went out walking," said Krysten. "We went down to the state park one day. Yeah we did. We'd take walks."

"And you drove me to meet Ryan," I said, laughing, "for the first time!"

"That was something I was wondering if you were even going to bring up!" said Krysten. "I did! And I dropped you off!"

"Yes you did!" I laughed. "And you came back a few hours later!"

"Well, we won't mention that to your man . . . I'm just teasing!" laughed Krysten. "I was like, 'Did I do the right thing?' But I picked you up after, I did. I'm still not sure, but you're a grown woman! But it was touchy that way. Yeah, you're grown, so you did your own thing. And you'd have let me know if you needed help."

"It's like when you took me to that wedding reception," I said. "Down at the club Medusa."

"For me," said Krysten, "that night, I was there, but you didn't need me around. I just picked you up and drove you, but you had a lot of good friends there. I was with my husband, and we kind of did our own thing. We even left and went for a walk. You had a great time! I know, when we picked you up, you sure were!"

"You're completely different now," said Krysten. "Not completely, I mean. You're still you, but I can tell. You were really childlike when I first met you. Oh, the Aflac duck commercial! That would come on, and for like three days, you had to talk about that. You'd crack up, over and over. That's all you talked about days, the Aflac duck.

"You slept a lot. You felt really nauseous a lot. You weren't really a complainer, which kind of really blew my mind because, I mean, everything that you'd gone through, really. You'd say when you were uncomfortable, but you wouldn't complain like I would have. You kept a good sense of humor, and that you still have today. You certainly like to laugh. You did then too!"

"Yes I did," I replied. "Yes I did."

"You use a cane now," observed Krysten. "You weren't ready to do that then."

"It wasn't until I met other people that were blind," I said, "and then I said, 'Fine. I'll try that.'"

"You got defiant about some things, maybe," said Krysten. "But that's just your personality, and that you are going to do things when you're ready to do them. You know, whatever it was. You only used my help as much as you needed me, but mostly, I just think we were friends.

"I remember we'd do beading. That was fun because I liked you to tell me the colors that you wanted. That was fun for a while, but then it was boring. I mean, how many beads are you gonna string in your life or whatever, you know?

"And so now, you know now that I'm not with you as much, I can tell, just seeing you sitting here, you're more comfortable. Not that you weren't comfortable with yourself then, but you are more, like, confident maybe? Not that you weren't then. You always have had that, I'm pretty sure that's something you've always had."

"I have," I said, "but now that I don't have a—quote, unquote—'guardian,' and I have my own place, and my house is clean and not covered with stuff everywhere—that drove me nuts! How often did I want to clean at that house?"

"I know you did too," Krysten said. "Remember we made the little box for your shoes to put under your bed? So you could keep your shoes dust-free under the bed in a little special box that you could slide in and out and keep them all in order. You are very organized! Oh my gosh, yes, your panty drawer even. I remember you going through that, and everything had to be laid out just so. You don't even fold them. They're just laid out like they would be on the Victoria's Secret shelf! It was good. You would talk to me about you don't need clutter. If a T-shirt is, like, a year old and it's hasn't got anything, not even a stitch missing, it's out!"

"Oh yeah," I replied.

"You've got more control over that now, I guess," said Krysten. "That's a good thing. Every girl's panty drawer should be—"

"Kept in order!" I interjected. "That's right. That's right."

"Another thing you did," said Krysten, "is that you're the first person I ever met that kept the volume on the radio down low enough that you could hear yourself sing. So we did that, we sang together in the car, and you told me that my voice wasn't *bad*. I'm trying to think, did we do anything extraordinary? Not really."

"It was just so many different things here and there," I said. "You taking me to get my haircut, shopping, grocery shopping with you for your family and with me."

"I don't remember, did you stay in my house very much?" asked Krysten.

"I did," I said. "Definitely for the one summer. I was there one or two nights a week for the whole summer pretty much."

"I bought a blow-up bed," laughed Krysten, "because I didn't want to sleep in my bedroom anyway. Were you there when Mitch said every time I blew up the air bed, it sounded like I was hammering the nails in the coffin of our marriage? I don't know if you want this to go in the book, but it was pretty funny. It was just drama."

"Drama!" I exclaimed, laughing.

"It was drama," repeated Krysten. "I'm just glad you can eat now, because that was a hard thing for you, honey. Everybody felt bad. You had to push food in through that little space."

"After my last jaw surgery," I said, "the first thing I had was a Philly cheesesteak. What was weird was I got a salad with that, and it was 'Wow! I forgot what this was like!'"

"You didn't use utensils too much," said Krysten. "There was no purpose. It was hard for me to see you go through that. I didn't feel pity or anything like that, it was more just 'Wow, this person's been through this,' and I was so amazed, everybody was, at what a good attitude you have, and how really most days you were just funny! You made me laugh more than anybody. What a great experience to get to spend time with somebody like you and be friends. It wasn't work! And I still—you know the way you'd hold my arm, the way that lady taught us—I still do that. There was this older gentleman I was working for, and he was getting to where he couldn't walk, but he didn't want his walker, and it came very naturally for me to do that again.

"And I still too—when the lights are out, I think about you. I know that might sound strange, but the way I watched you get around in my house—you would always use the back of your hand to feel things. And you could hear everything! And do you still cook?"

"You should come out to our house," I said. "I don't cook as much, but that's because our friend Dave comes over, and he's an awesome chef."

"So you're not having to cook at all then," said Krysten. "You've got a barbecue and a chef and a great kitchen."

"Oh, I still like to cook sometimes," I said. "Sometimes I just like to prepare because I love the big island that we have in our kitchen. So I'll be chopping this and that, and I'll pass it to him at the stove, and we'll go back and forth."

"Do you love your house?" asked Krysten.

"Yessss!" I responded, proudly. "Everything is up to snuff and just right. Also, the last time I saw you, I had a Jeep Grand Cherokee. But last week, did I tell you what happened?"

"You had several things go wrong with your Jeep," said Krysten.

"Well, the first thing that happened, I'd only had it a month, and we're walking out of Rita's, my aesthetician, and we go out, and the back end is smashed in. Someone smashed it in and left no note, no nothing. Just smashed in the back end. We get that fixed, and then three months later, we're at the ferry terminal, waiting to get across, and someone in front of us just backed up without looking and smashed in the front end! And then two weeks ago, we're driving to my aesthetician, and a big rock slams into the windshield. So I was like, 'Okay, that's it with this one.' It obviously has some bad Jeep juju, so we need to get rid of it. So I traded it in, and I got a Jeep Wrangler four door. It's army green, so I decided to name it Sargent."

"What do you remember about the time we spent together, Maria?" asked Krysten.

"I just remember that when I was with you, I felt like I was doing something," I answered. "I felt really relaxed and comfortable with you. We could just talk about whatever—because we did talk about *whatever.*"

"We did," replied Krysten.

"I just remember being very comfortable," I continued. "I will say the person I got after you left—she was nice and everything, but it wasn't the same at all."

"She was a nice lady," said Krysten. "She was older though. She was a hippie, and you and I were closer in age."

"She was way too hippie for me!" I responded. "And she was the sort of person that believed that you shouldn't use deodorant or antiperspirant, you rub crystals under your arms! And I'm thinking, 'What the hell? What the hell are we doing here!' She is a really neat lady, and she worked hard for me, but that's something I just don't get. Crystals in the armpits. All righty then."

Krysten laughed, and then I said, "Hey, we're going to do karaoke tonight! I think I've told you before, I'm sure I have. The song that Rob first sang for karaoke was 'Big Balls' by AC/DC. He does the accent perfectly, and I swear to god, when I heard him sing it, I thought they were playing the CD! I'm like, 'How the hell do you do that?' And oh, the way he does Ray Charles—we had fun with that the other night! He borrowed some dark sunglasses and my white cane, and he had a friend of ours lead him up to the stage. Then he sang 'Georgia on My Mind.'"

"That's funny!" laughed Krysten.

"It gets even funnier," I continued. "When he got offstage, a woman asked if he was making fun of blind people, but then she met me, and she understood everything!"

"That's *really* funny!" Krysten said, laughing again.

"I know." I laughed in return. "You should come with us tonight!"

"Sounds like fun!" Krysten replied.

RITA

Since my accident, my skin has had problems beyond those of teenagers. As a result, I've spent a lot of time going to my aesthetician, Rita. The ladies in my family have gone to her for years and lovingly refer to her as Rita the German Zitpicker. On a recent visit, I spoke with her about our experiences together.

"I was going to tell you something that I learned from the paramedic," I said, "and I thought you'd appreciate this. I learned from the paramedic when I was talking with him for this book. At the hospital, when I was there that night—I'd never heard this before, and I don't even think my family has heard this—the one thing I did after they were thinking I was done and they were prepping me for organ donation—"

"Ja, I think you told me," said Rita.

"No, no," I said. "This is different. Because I had heard that I had pushed the nurse away. Guess what else I did!"

"You kicked them," guessed Rita.

"No," I said. "Watch my arm. I did this." I raised my arm and put my hand toward my face, trying to feel it. "And I started touching my face. When the paramedic was telling me this, he reached over and touched my hand, and he said, 'Is this okay to tell you?' And I said, 'Yeah, I was probably just checking to make sure my mascara hadn't run!'"

Rita and I both laughed.

"That's Maria for you!" Rita proclaimed. "See? And that's what I wanted to say when you told me that. What impressed me the most was your sense of humor, and you are so positive about life, and everybody could learn from you. You! You people who have less hardships to go through could learn from this! Well, when you first came here, your face had never been, in my opinion, never been washed since you went through the hospital. Your face was so . . . how would I say? Crusty! And you had breakouts all over. It was bad!

"But I was scared to touch you! Because I didn't want to hurt you! And I didn't know, you know, I'd never experienced anything like it! But look at your skin now!"

"No, I know," I replied. "One of the problems I had was the condition of my lips. I had to keep putting stuff on them."

"Don't put Vaseline on them. It cracks them even more!" said Rita. "Olive oil!"

"It kind of works for a lot of things, doesn't it?" I replied.

"Ja, you're Italian," said Rita. "I was so concerned that I might not be able to do what you needed, you know, because it was so bad. And you passed glass through your skin and bone splinters."

"And you could even smell when there was infection coming about, right?" I asked.

"Ja," said Rita. "I could tell you. Ja."

"I remember you saying it out loud to me before too," I said.

"Ja. Your sinus infection," said Rita. "Ja, and I went through you getting new eyes. You told me how they painted exactly like yours. I mean, for me, it was such a positive experience because you are such a positive person. And you could kick anybody up! You know. And every time you come in, we just laugh!"

"You said I passed a lot of glass," I said, slyly setting her up for another joke.

"Ja, glass splinters?" asked Rita.

"So when I'd fart, they'd shatter, right?" I said.

Rita laughed heartily. "There we go again!" she said, as she laughed some more. After catching her breath, she went on. "Oh, what else can I say? You came once a week and look at now! I'm really impressed. Even your chin!" she said cutely. "It gets better! And you told me about this doctor who gives you a total new face. Remember that?"

"Yeah," I said, smiling.

"Yeah," she said in a loving way. "And your eyebrows are still as beautiful as they were, and that's very important in a face. I have to dye mine!"

"When I was meeting with the paramedic, when he came over to my house," I said, "he told me what happened to my face—and I didn't really realize. I know it got smashed in, but I guess my skin literally just got totally impaled. It got curled up and flipped back. But that's how the skin stayed so perfect, and I've only got a scar here and a scar here, is it literally just flayed it open, and it flipped back like pie dough, you know? Very interesting."

"Ja. The furniture hit you right here, with the corner," said Rita, touching my scars. "Okay, close your lips," Rita commanded, as she applied treatment mask. As she worked, we continued to reminisce. "How long have you been coming to me?" asked Rita.

"Oh, it's been—" I said, thinking back, "I think I started coming in '05?"

"Wow," said Rita.

"I think it was about a year and a couple months after the accident," I said.

"And then I met all your caretakers," said Rita. "You know, the girls. And then I met all your boyfriends. The blind guy, who turned out to be a . . . and the parents were bad! And they ate junk food, and you were into health food."

"Well, at least something normal," I said. "It's not like the parents were only into it, it's just that they were always kind of 'Whatever,' and that's all he wanted. Drove me nuts."

"And that other guy that was so mean," said Rita. "I met him, who stole from you!"

"Yeah, he was never mean to me," I replied. "He just ended up being an ass wipe with what he did."

"He was here," said Rita. "But then you met your honey bunny! And it was such a good choice!" Rita exclaimed. "And then your puppies! You brought always your puppies in. And I remember you saying you adopted Nick, because . . . what's the expression . . . Because he is old and decrepit . . . You said you are all special, and that's why you adopted him! Because we are all cripples or something—that's your sense of humor, anyway. So Ja, I have good memories, and I tell everybody. Not directly, but I say, 'You should see a friend of mine, who is totally blind, and how she handles life, and that I have learned to be positive about not whining.' Gosh, and I hear so many people whining! Ah, include my daughter! Oh my God!"

"Well, I think that's all," said Rita, as she finished my treatment. "I am amazed how your skin came. How beautiful it is now. Ja," she said, very satisfied.

MACARONI AND BUTTERFLIES

As I said before, I lost a lot of time, but you cannot imagine where I've been, where that's concerned. People get drunk and wake up places, not knowing where they are, why they're there, or what happened. I know that. I'm a bartender. Don't think I haven't heard the stories.

Try trying to wake up after taking a board to the face through your windshield, with other people shoving drugs into your system for months on end. Just try that.

And no, I don't want your sympathy.

Sympathy is defined in the dictionary as "feelings of pity and sorrow for someone else's misfortune." I don't want your pity or your sorrow. Fuck that shit.

Meanwhile, *empathy* is defined as "the ability to understand and share the feelings of another." That's why I'm writing this book. Therefore, I hope you'll at least try to understand me and where I've been and what I've been through. I want to share this with you. And I hope you never have to go there.

Hey, I studied communications. I'm trying to communicate with you. Obviously, you're reading this, and you've bothered to make it this far. So—so far, so good. But there is a part of me that still wants to shout at the top of my lungs, "Sit down and shut the fuck up! Quit being nice to me! I need you to know what went on and what's going on!"

And now, permit me to draw a deep breath before continuing.

After all, I did get a bachelor's degree in communications, and I had dedicated myself to understanding that well enough to teach the subject. So forgive me for not being nice about having a thing to say. Too many people, well-intentioned or otherwise, got in my face when they wanted me to communicate in the way they expected and desired. All I wanted was for them to listen, in the broader sense of the term. I wanted them to listen on all frequencies, as it were. I wanted them to "hear." More importantly, I wanted them to tell me what was going on. I didn't know, and that bit of information, as painful as it might have been, might have made a world of difference to me.

You might remember the movie *The Right Stuff.* If not, you should see it. It's February 20, 1962, and John Glenn is in orbit, and mission control is trying to figure out how to tell John Glenn that his heat shield might have disengaged before it should have. They can't think of how to tell him that. Thousands of people at mission control, and nobody knows what to say.

Sure, I know it's Hollywood. But at least this part of Hollywood is based on real life. I know that nothing is as simple as what you see on the silver screen, but sometimes art imitating life needs to be taken to heart. According to both the book and the movie, what did Alan Shepard say?

"He's a pilot. You tell him the condition of his craft."

Nobody ever told me that. Forty-two years after John Glenn's spaceflight, and I'm in the same situation: no one's able to figure out how to tell me what's going on.

Yes, I have to rely on the memory of friends, relatives, and the professionals who saved my life to fill in the gaps. You wouldn't think any different if someone had passed out for a moment by traveling to the farthest reaches of space or diving to the depths of the sea. Hell, I've been a bartender, and some of you that are reading this have blacked out in front of me. What do you do when that happens? You revive them, and you're happy they make it back to consciousness.

In my case, of course—and thank goodness that some of them were good people—no matter the cost.

So yes, sure, you might even welcome an astronaut or deep-sea diver or a climber from the summit of K2 or Mount Everest as a hero for making it back from the brink of death; trust me, all the "hero" wants in those circumstances is just to be alive.

I've never done anything but want to live life to the fullest. So never, never, never treat me like I'm not the master of my own body, let alone of my ongoing existence. At the same time, please do respect that I'm not only trying to communicate some things to you but also that I was studying communications, wanting to teach others how to do it, when this madness happened to me.

So.

Now let me tell you what I do remember.

I was coming home from work—or so I'm told—and suddenly, the next thing I know is that I'm stuck in a room, tied to a bed, and nobody will turn the lights on or tell me why they won't let me go or why the lights are off.

"Who the hell is touching me! Back off!" is all I want to say. And trust me, long before I could say it, my face ripped off by someone's entertainment center, I dropped the F-bomb more than I care to consider.

To me, it was all a weird dream. I wanted to sleep, but I wanted to do that for so long. I'd worked so hard, but no one would let me sleep. All this poking and prodding. People wanting things from me. I kept telling them no.

There are more things in life than words. There's this thing called body language. I'm no psychologist like my dad, but I learned a lot about that from him, and I learned a lot about that as a bartender. Most people can't say everything with their mouths. Well, they could if they were well-spoken and had an audience that understood them, but there are some times in everyone's life that—fuck, I'm sure that even Shakespeare was at a loss for words at times.

So yeah. I had my face torn off with a board that came through my windshield. Imagine that.

Seriously, imagine that.

Of course, everyone is thrilled and happy that after all that, you're still alive. They're happy you haven't left them. They want you to get better. They want to help you heal.

And during all that—I find it funny now, and I'm sure I was relieved then—all I could say was "macaroni and butterflies" when I wanted macaroni and cheese. As a student of communications, I love that I said that. There's nothing wrong with saying a thing you mean when people finally understand what you're trying to say.

But as you've already heard, the first thirsty words I spoke were that I wanted a Coke. My face smashed in, a tracheotomy tube down my neck—I'm sure I didn't know what the hell had happened to me then. I'd done more than win the Super Bowl or survive a heavyweight prizefight, but I sure as hell didn't want to go to Disneyland. I just wanted a cool, refreshing fizzy drink.

Who the hell wouldn't?

Tubes in my body, totally blind, but no one has the courage to tell me so. Of course, I tried to escape like Houdini—and the nurses called me that! Did they not think I was listening? As a bartender and server, I learned to listen with my ears. Even though I didn't know what the hell was going on, I knew how to try to figure out what the hell was going on. I wanted out! I got my hands out of the restraints, I removed IVs—I did everything I could do to escape the madness.

Of course, nobody thinks you're listening. People assume that in restaurants. People assume that in bars. Trust me, a professional hears it. You think that you're whispering, but even if most of the words are missing, you can still receive the message inadvertently. It's kind of like removing all the vowels from a sentence; you can still read it. I guess that's why you have to "buy" a vowel on *Wheel of Fortune*, right?

So yeah, I was drugged up—the same sort of drugged up that almost killed me had the neurologist not taken the interest to ask, and the nurses inadvertently to say, that when I was off that paralytic drug derived from the jellyfish, I actually did try to see what the fuck was going on. Hell yeah, I reached for my face! I hadn't been able to do so since I left work! And by the way, hospital food bites, especially since you're feeding me and I can't taste anything.

Do you think I didn't hear about the organ donorship that almost happened after the fact? Or that you had to live through a "bereavement package" and get sent home? Sure, not at the time, but I heard you through the mist of what was going on afterward. Through the haze of drugs administered to me, of course I knew something of what was going on, and I heard a lot of what you said.

After a while, things began to make sense. Sort of. I was still on other people's drugs. Way too many of them. Not everybody knows how to deal with things, especially if they've been put on drugs they didn't ask for. In my case, I wanted out—out of the darkness, out from under the influence of the drugs, out of the information blackout.

One of the first things I could communicate with was music, song lyrics to be precise. I knew all the words, and I could sing along. No problem. And of course, as Krysten later experienced, as always I preferred, the music was turned down low enough so that I could hear myself sing along.

Of course, nobody who has a long story to tell ever tells it all in the order of the events as they happened. I studied communications, so at least trust me on that; and if you can't, at least acknowledge that Hollywood gets away with it frequently and that you like it when they do it that way. They make money and win Oscars based on nonsequential storytelling. Do I have to go *Wayne's World* on your ass to make my point? "Doodladooo, doodladoo, doodladoo, doodladoo." You like it. I know that you do.

So first, let me tell you about all the medical aspects of my experience. When you're sick or injured, you really need your sleep; but it's really hard to sleep with lots of staples in your head especially if you're like me and you like to sleep on your side. There was simply no way that I could do that, and I had to sleep on my back, and let me tell you, I didn't get much sleep that way.

And then of course there were the drugs. After everything I've been through, I can't understand why anyone would take prescription drugs for fun. Oxycodone was the worst. All that stuff does is make you drool and put your brain in a perpetual haze. It's hard enough to deal with a traumatic accident and lose your eyesight. I swear at least half of my problems were based on being overprescribed painkillers and antipsychotics and all sorts of whatever. Sure, I'm sure the doctors had good intentions, but I wonder if my recovery might have gone a whole lot faster if they'd cut back on the chemistry a little bit, or maybe even a lot, and let me have some input regarding my medication needs.

And through it all, the doctors kept going on and on about what my limitations were going to be. Really? Me? Limitations? Even though I still wasn't sure what had happened and my head was fogged in with a smog of prescription drugs, I wasn't going to have any of that, so I just wanted them to shut up about that and point me in the direction I wanted to go: out of there and on with my life!

People were telling me I was blind, but I didn't understand. They were telling me I'd been in an accident, but I didn't remember anything about my accident. Sure, I've still got some memory loss about the accident, but I might have caught on to my situation, especially my blindness, a little quicker without all the damn drugs!

Of course, there was a whole battery of surgeries and procedures to endure: surgery to stop the bleeding, surgery to remove necrotic flesh, surgery to harvest bone from my hip and to rebuild my face, surgery for temple implants and my nose, surgery to reduce scars, surgery to remove my braces, more surgery on my nose, surgery to remove what was left of my right eye, getting a prosthetic eye to replace my right eye, procedures to decide about my left eye and surgery to have it removed when the doctors deemed there was no hope there, Getting a pair of prosthetic eyes made, and surgery to reduce my upper lip.

Then there were the tubes. Tubes, tubes, tubes, and more tubes—tubes to drain this, tubes to drain that, tubes to feed me with. When I went in have surgery to have my braces removed, they waited until after the anesthesia wore off to pull out my tummy tube. What was the purpose of that? Of course, it had been in there for months, and my body had a pretty good grip on it. All that tugging and pain and then the local anesthesia, when they just could have done it when I was under for the surgery. Makes me wonder sometimes.

There were the so-called occupational therapy classes I had to take. As an example, let me tell you about the dreaded coffee-cup exercises, which is little more than to reach into a coffee cup and pull things out to identify, like coins, paper clips, and so on. My attitude about this was one of "duh-duh-dee, duh-duh-dee . . . treat me like I'm stupid." I'm sure, to them, they thought they were helping; after all, I had trouble doing it. The whole time, however, I wanted to shout, "Get me off these damn drugs, and I'll do a lot better at this bullshit!" But I couldn't; I was too high on the damn drugs!

There was getting driven places as a passenger—a blind passenger. A blind passenger on a lot of damn prescription drugs. I hated it. Sure, I'd get nauseous, and I didn't like it, but not for the reasons you might think. It's apparently true what people say about women and stick shifts; most just can't do it. I would get carsick, and it was almost always a woman driving when that happened. The only women that managed stick shifts without making me sick were my aunt Susan and Aunt Liz. Other than that, bring on the barf bag!

I'm sure I was no picnic for the more sensitive ears around me. When every other word you say is *fuck*, I suppose it gets really old to the other people after a while, even if you don't find the word offensive. The words *is, and, but, the*, and *fuck* were about the only vocabulary I seemed to have for a long time. Again, I blame the drugs as much as anything. They lower your inhibitions, just like alcohol does. As a result, I had a bit of a problem not proclaiming how horny I was and how much I needed sex—albeit not as nicely as that—while I was in the hospital. No, I was considerably more vulgar than that, and I'm sure I made a lot of male orderlies blush.

One day I noticed a spot in my lip that really hurt. I made an appointment with my surgeon to check it out. Lo and behold, out came a piece of my windshield!

Things still work their way to the surface of my face from time to time. Where would I be without my aesthetician, good ol' Rita "the German Zitpicker," the Dr. Ruth of skin care. After the accident and all the surgery, my skin was constantly breaking out something fierce. I knew. I didn't need working eyes and a mirror to know that. Stuff got so messed up in there, under the skin in my face. More than just the damage to my skin, I had other problems. My hormones were all out of whack, for instance. It was like going through puberty all over again.

And from time to time, quite frequently in fact, something I thought was a pimple or a whitehead would turn out to be one of the many tiny bits of glass that would come to the surface of my skin, like a splinter working its way out. It took a long time for my skin to clear up. I'm glad I had Rita to help me with all that.

My Social Life

During my lengthy recovery, people that I used to work with would come around to visit me. I enjoyed that. It was nice. I found myself picturing them when they were talking with me; the way their eyes would sparkle or the way they'd smile would be playing in my head as they talked. I knew the expressions on their faces just by listening to them.

Of course, I made every effort to get out and about as much as I could. On my twenty-fifth birthday, the first since my accident, we went out on the town in a limo. My friends and family took me to Club Medusa. It was late October and pretty cold out. By the time we got into the club, I was sitting there with a chill and shivering a little and my head pounding with a migraine. One of my girlfriends knew exactly how to cure that though; she brought me a martini! That solved the problem! Warmed up, migraine gone, I was ready to dance! So dance I did! My aunt Liz was there, and I remember her saying, "Shake your moneymaker!" There I was, only eight months after my accident, and I was out having the time of my life, living again. It felt so good to leave all my troubles behind and just dance, dance, dance.

I was plagued with migraines in those days, and anything that would give me relief from them was wonderful. The drugs I was on weren't giving me any real relief. I found that lifting weights and exercising helped make them go away. I got a personal trainer after I got out of the hospital. Her name was Tracy, and we ended up becoming friends and hanging out and having fun. We'd hang out at Medusa or at her house. And getting out to the gym was good for me because I got to be out in the world again and meet people. And unlike the hospital, where they talked at me, people talked with me!

And of course, there was always retail therapy at Nordstrom Rack! That helped the migraines too! The Mother Ship to the rescue, as always.

After turning twenty-five, I was feeling the need to date again. Let's face it, I'd been out of circulation for a while, and I needed to get some action! Or at least go out with someone. Not dating can make a person crazy. Community services for the blind was helpful in this; they helped blind people meet, and they hooked me up with Ryan, who had lost his eyesight too. I guess you can say I finally went on a "blind" date. It was good to be around someone my own age to talk and bullshit with. It was nice to be around another person who was dealing with some of the same changes in life as well.

Ryan was living with his parents at the time, and I would go over to their house for weekend visits. Again, it was nice to get away from the cabin and be around people who liked to do fun things. They had Yahtzee with dice that had external dots, and we played that for hours. In the mornings, Ryan's dad would go to Starbucks and bring back coffee and breakfast. Ah, a Starbucks and a morning cigarette—glorious.

Ryan and I were in a two-year relationship. He proposed to me, and I said yes. Like many engagements, there was an announcement in the newspaper, which was followed by an article about us. As a result, E. E. Robbins, a local jewelry store, gave us an engagement ring on the house. It didn't work out in the long run, and we broke up, but it was a good experience.

I went to a couple of weddings, one to attend and one as a bridesmaid. I started hanging out with former coworkers and started dating again. More and more, I started feeling the most normal ever!

The Legal Stuff

The medical bills from all this were, of course, huge. My family sought help from Washington State Crime Victims Compensation, which was established to help people who have suffered personal injury from a violent crime with the associated costs; but what happened to me, as violent as it was, wasn't technically a criminal act.

Of course, they guy that was incompetently hauling the entertainment center in an open trailer only got slapped on the wrist for failing to secure a load, driving without insurance, driving with a suspended license, and littering. They fined him about $1,000 and let him go.

My family then talked to attorneys, and they recommended seeking damages from the company that had rented him the trailer. I knew there was going to be a legal thing that was going to start happening. At some point, I even met with the attorneys, or should I say that they met with me? Because as I've said repeatedly, the doctors had me so doped up on prescriptions I wasn't really part of the process.

When all the court stuff started, I felt like a prisoner on lockdown in my own home. Reporters were everywhere, all day and night, practically camping on the doorstep. Just like in the movies, reporters tried every trick in the book to gain access to me. They'd open the gate without permission and try to get in the house. I remember one reporter saying, "Oh, I've talked with her before!" as if that was some sort of backstage pass. Look, folks, I know there's a story here, but really? Can we act like we have some manners please? In a word—pushy!

As far as the trial itself, which was about a two-week process, I only went to court once; and that was the time I got up on the stand to testify. Other than that, I really wasn't involved.

This was all going on in late October 2007. Pretty soon, it was my birthday again. My friend Mason called me and wanted to go out to celebrate my twenty-eighth a few days late, so on November 4, we went to Belltown to see old friends. While we were out enjoying our evening, it was the top-news story; the media got in on the air before the attorneys could even get out of the courthouse. The jury found for me.

Finally it was over.

The defendants, of course, immediately filed for an appeal, as usually happens in such cases, but I was glad to have the trial over with. All these people arguing over me!

The fat lady didn't sing until the following spring, when my attorneys and I had a mediation with the defense. An agreement was reached in one day. That's when things really felt good. At last, all that nonsense was over and done.

My Great-Grandmother

My great-grandma Kitty was a big part of my life. I remember everything about her house and how it was decorated. I remember the big TV and watching when the I-90 bridge sank in the storm. She watched Lawrence Welk every Sunday and *Wheel of Fortune* and *Jeopardy* every night. I remember her playing cribbage and that she made the best chocolate-chip cookies ever! I remember how we'd walk to the Husky Deli for ice cream and candy when I was little girl.

When I didn't have to be somewhere else, I was almost always at Grandma Kitty's.

By the time of the trial, Grandma Kitty was living in a nursing home. She always had pictures of me everywhere, and she always made me feel like I was her favorite great-granddaughter.

I'm told she passed away the same day of the verdict from the trial.

I remember going to her funeral about a week after the verdict. It was the first and only funeral I've ever been to.

Who would have thought that such a thing would happen? What timing.

I remember my aunt Liz baked those delicious cookies for the funeral. That meant a lot to everybody. It meant a lot to me.

That's the real stuff I remember from then. Not the trial, not the verdict, just that Grandma Kitty passed away.

My Home Life

Back when I got out of Good Samaritan, after all that time in the hospital, I moved to the cabin my grandparents bought for their summers on Lake Kathleen. Living at "home," getting around with no cane, caregivers carting me about for various appointments, still in "what accident?" mode because I was pumped full of too many drugs, I tried the best I could to get back to living my life.

My mom was there, and I remember she tended to watch just two movies over and over: *An Officer and a Gentleman* and *Pretty Woman*. Really? Can we expand our taste in movies please? There are a lot more movies out there.

She wouldn't let me use the stove. "You'll burn the house down!" she'd say tersely. After all those years of relying on me to prepare her food and be her housekeeper, and I'm not allowed in the kitchen.

Well, I embrace my Italian ancestry, right? And I'm stuck with some woman who just doesn't get it. Her idea of Italian cuisine is Prego. Really? Really? That's all we have? Under such limitations, what's a girl to do? Get inventive, that's what. So I learned to make pasta in the microwave in a glass bowl and try my best to sauce up the Prego with whatever I could lay my hands on.

It was tough going there for a while. Fortunately, people like Krysten did their best to get me some normalcy by letting me stay at their homes on occasion, do the things I was capable of and even things a little beyond, trusting me to fail, pick myself up, and try again like any adult.

After the verdict, I was able to rent the house next door. That helped out quite a bit. For the first time, I finally had a closet big enough for all my clothes. I still had people coming over to take me to appointments and do things like go grocery shopping, but at last, I had the independence I'd been craving since waking up in the hospital.

After living there a while, I started dating a guy that worked as a cook. Even though I couldn't smell much, it was fun to have someone come visit and cook for me!

Out on My Own

After the accident, I was put under a full guardianship. I understand why this was done, but then again I don't. Sure, there were things that needed to be done and decisions to be made. Eventually, this was changed to a limited guardianship in 2009, and in 2010, a judge finally ruled that I was able to take care of my own business, and the limited guardianship was terminated.

I have to wonder if all that was really necessary. Aren't family members allowed to make medical decisions when one is incapacitated? Wouldn't a simple power of attorney have sufficed for everything else? Sign the consent forms and get me fixed up, take care of my personal business on my behalf while I'm on the mend, and then let me decide when I'm ready to take control of things again.

I don't know. I'm not a lawyer, but I'm not going to go spend money answering that question. The guardianship thing is water under the bridge now. I'm just thinking that if the doctors had been a little less happy with their prescription pads and if people had had a little more confidence in me getting through it all, then all that legal stuff wouldn't have been necessary. I'm just curious, that's all. Like always, I like to figure things out and ponder stuff.

Either way, that didn't stop me! Even while I was still on a full guardianship, a friend of the family picked me up and drove me around so that I could start shopping for a home. I like West Seattle. I grew up there. Among the things I like are the simpler pleasures, like local shops to go to and sidewalks to get there. It's quiet and pleasant and away from the hustle and bustle of Seattle. It's my kind of community. It's my kind of place to call home.

So I went house shopping in West Seattle. I found this quaint little ninety-year-old house that I fell in love with. It needed a lot of work, but it was just adorable. Since anything I was going to buy would need modifications to accommodate a blind lifestyle, I thought the old house and I were a perfect match.

Now when I say the old house needed a lot of work, I mean just that—it needed a lot of work. Basically, it had been to be gutted and rebuilt. But as I said, this was a perfect opportunity. The house had been gutted and rebuilt with the interior opened up, eliminating all the unnecessary little rooms and doorways connecting them—all the stuff that presents unnecessary difficulties, whether or not you're blind.

In 2008 it was mostly ready, and I moved into my first home. I'd finally gotten there. After having all my plans—my entire life—interrupted, I finally had one plan come to fruition: a home of my own, a place to live.

+

I can tell you, there was this overwhelming sense of satisfaction of finally being where I wanted to be.

After I had moved in, my dad came to visit. Dad and I went to Husky Deli for old times' sake. While we were there, an older woman said, "I know you!" *Oh no,* I thought to myself, *not another as-seen-on-TV moment!* But then she said, "I remember when you came in here as a little girl," and she told me about the days when my grandma Kitty and I would come there to buy ice cream.

That made it nice to be in West Seattle. I was finally home.

Jaw Surgery

The "experts" said that I would never walk, talk, hear, blink, work my jaw, or breathe though my nose. Of course, they were wrong on all counts.

For instance, my uncle Richard is a professional billiards player. Of course, you can learn a lot about basic physics by playing pool. He's a practical guy. What the experts were saying simply didn't make sense to him, and he wasn't about to take the word of medical professionals on anything he could verify for himself. So he took a tissue and let a corner of it dangle in front of my nose. Of course, the air moving in and out of my nose moved the tissue back and forth. With a simple, practical test, he showed the doctors what was what.

For a long time, I wondered what could be done about my jaw. I'd been through an extensive regimen of rehabilitation exercises intended to increase my range of motion. It hadn't worked. My guy, Rob, who I'd been with for a few years at that point, encouraged me to keep looking for answers. I went to an oral surgeon. He didn't know what could be done, so he went on a mission to find someone who would know what to do. He found the right specialist in Spokane and forwarded my medical records, which by this time were over three hundred pages!

He agreed to see me, so in April 2010, I flew to Spokane. First, he ran an open-MRI head scan on me. That's when he saw things he'd never seen before. Apparently, underneath my skin, I look like the Terminator, what with all the titanium used to reconstruct my skull. He was floored!

He noticed that a lot of major nerves that he was used to seeing in MRI scans didn't show up. So he did a pin test to check my reflexes and ability to feel. He had me squint one eye at a time, blink, and raise my eyebrows. He was astonished again, because without those nerves I shouldn't be able to do all that.

The MRI exposed that parts of the reconstructive surgery were interfering, banging into each other. This was the real reason I couldn't open my jaw. Nine hours of surgery later, he'd removed some small metal parts through a small incision in front of my left ear.

Coming out of surgery, groggily, I said, "Look at me!" and stuck out my tongue. After the surgery, the nurse took me to the bathroom and gave me a toothbrush. Amazing! For the first time in years, I could brush my teeth!

With the surgery and recovery, we were there for a whole week. We flew home to Seattle and then flew back to Spokane a week later for a follow-up visit with the doctor. While we were there, we went to lunch, and I ordered a Philly cheesesteak sandwich and a Caesar salad. What a thrill it was to eat a tasty Caesar salad again and eat it with a fork! Yummy.

Of course, as you've read earlier, I never really lost my sense of humor through all that's happened. But after the jaw surgery, I could really feel my sense of humor return in full, along with a sense of what I'd accomplished in overcoming so many obstacles and challenges. So while in Spokane, I turned to my guy, Rob, and said with all my heart, "I'm glad the accident happened. I wouldn't have met you."

My Significant Other—Now Husband

One day, when I was still living at the cabin on Lake Kathleen, I was out shopping at an antique store. I met the owner. He was a really nice guy. His name is Rob.

Rob and I hung out and got along really well. On our first date, we went to dinner, went dancing, and got along great, talking about whatever. We didn't get home until five in the morning.

We started dating. Once, we went to the Fremont Solstice Day parade and enjoyed the grunge music that was being played. Rob told me about the naked guys that were there; they do that sort of thing on Solstice Day in Fremont. It's that kind of neighborhood and that kind of festival. Naked old guys. Yep, there are some benefits to being blind!

I like to sing. Sometimes I like to go to karaoke. I know all the words to "Baby Got Back" by Sir Mix-a-Lot, and it's fun to sing. I got Rob hooked on karaoke. He's become quite the karaoke performer since then, and nobody sings AC/DC's "Big Balls" like he does. He sounds just like the original record!

In 2009, it was meet-the-dad time! Dad liked how good we are for each other and gave us his blessing. He gave Rob his dad's wedding band, and he gave me the anniversary ring my grandfather gave to my grandmother so that we could commemorate our relationship.

We went on vacation to Italy and Greece. I'd been to British Columbia and Mexico, and I'd flown over water before when I went to visit my dad in Alaska and Hawaii. But this was the first time I'd really ever traveled out of the country.

We got off the plane, checked into the hotel, and immediately hit the streets! First, it was weird to find McDonald's everywhere; I mean I knew they were there, but it was weird to experience it firsthand. Why is my culture following me? I came here to experience yours! It didn't take long though to get past that and find what I was seeking.

I don't know about all this "ugly American tourist" stuff I've always heard of. We certainly didn't get treated like that. In fact, it was the complete opposite. We got treated exceptionally well. And oh, the antiquities! The museums! The architecture! Unlike anything I've ever experienced in the United States—they encouraged me to touch things. You may have been to Greece too, and you may have seen the Parthenon. I got to *touch* the

Parthenon. It wasn't that I was allowed to, they insisted. So I felt the columns of the Parthenon and touched the surface of stones that had witnessed thousands of years of history. It was amazing.

After we returned home, we called the Greek consulate to thank them for their hospitality.

I know we'll be back.

My Dogs

Dogs know. Dogs know a lot. Thank goodness for Sam, my first Cavalier King Charles spaniel. What is it that they say? If you want to know about a person, see how they're treated by dogs and kids. One of the best things that happened to me was Sammy. Only five months old, and he gets out of the car, never having met me, and he runs straight over and sits down on my feet. Not at my feet but on them. Sammy knew.

Sammy was born the day after my accident. It was about the same time as the call from Harborview calling everyone back to the hospital. At least that's what I'm told, and it might just be true. I'm not superstitious. I don't think that happened by some sort of grand design. Who's to know if it happened by chance? Maybe the breeder said so just because. Sometimes people go out of their way to make you feel special when something bad happens. After all, I was in the news, and people knew things. None of that really matters, does it? Sammy saw me, came to me, and loved me immediately. Say what you will; I just think he was—and still is—pretty fucking smart and compassionate. I wish most people could be as smart as Sam.

There is a thing called the Delta Society that trains and certifies service and therapy dogs. A lady from the Delta Society contacted me and helped me train Sam as a service dog. They tested him, and he passed with no problem. Sammy got his therapy badge!

I thought Sammy needed to have a friend, so we went on a trip in search of a pal for him. As they say among Cavalier King Charles spaniel fanciers, "To Cav or not to Cav, that is the question." When I met her, I knew her name; but I didn't say it. I just sat there, and all of a sudden, she came right to me and jumped on my lap. "Hi! I'm here!" she seemed to say. Her name was Sadie. She was being retired from breeding after delivering three litters. She was perfect, so home we went with Sadie, and Sam and Sadie have been pals ever since.

I still have a special place in my heart for Jack Russell terriers, and I have ever since I knew my aunt Susan's Jack Russell, Brewster, when I was a kid. So I decided to go to the Humane Society and see if I could find a Jack

Russell terrier to rescue. Cavalier King Charles spaniels are wonderful, loving dogs, but I thought they could use a little spice in their life in the form of a feisty Jack Russell.

When we got there, there was Nick. He's an older dog, and he'd been owned by an old woman who had moved to a retirement home. He was perfect too. We took him home, and he became our little Jack Russell "terrorist," keeping Sam and Sadie in line, especially when Sadie starts barking when she's not supposed to.

The one funny thing about Nick is that he doesn't like the sound of farts. Maybe it had something to do with his previous owner. All I know is that if you make a fart sound—real or imitated—Nick runs off with his tail between his legs! Zoom! Away he goes!

Back to Life

As you've read, I've had a lot to accomplish over the last several years. I've traveled a long road of recovery, found a house, and I've made a home for myself with my man and my pups. I'm an ambitious person, so of course my attitude is one of, "What's next?"

Well, what about bartending again? Perhaps to the uninitiated, that might seem quite a stretch for a blind person to undertake; but if you've ever worked as a bartender or if you've ever taken the time to observe, there's a lot less sight involved than you think. Liquor is kept in a rail, and in most bars, the order of the bottles is the same. Even if it isn't, and in other places, like the top shelf, all the bottles are different shapes. It's an unintended benefit of product identity and branding that I can tell which is what. The same goes for beer in bottles or on tap; they're all in a particular place in the refrigerator or on the wall, and bottles and tap handles also vary by brand and product. There's no real issue there. Glassware? Same thing. Usually stacked in order by type, consistently in the same place—like I couldn't do that, right?

If a blind person can find all eighty-eight keys on a piano, I think you'll agree that some bottles in a rail, a few buttons on a soda gun, and a rack of glasses really don't pose that much of a challenge. I'm used to taking drink orders verbally and keeping track of all that. Also, I'm a great conversationalist. People like to talk to their bartenders. It's a traditional part of the job.

Sure, there are limitations. I can't check IDs, and doing things like running credit cards poses a bit of a problem the way the world currently does things. Other than that, there's no real reason I can't be an effective member of a team.

Which is why I've already done something about that. I've been "guest bartending" at some local restaurants and taverns, and it's worked out just fine. In fact, people dig it.

To my knowledge, I'm the only blind bartender in Washington, perhaps even in America. A local TV news program did a story on me, and the video went viral. It even ended up on an Italian bartending website. I haven't heard of anything like that in the news or on the web. I may not be the only one, but if I'm not unique, at the very least, bartenders like me are rare.

However, I never intended to be a bartender for life. That's why I went to college and got a communications degree. Now that I've got a lot of the shit that happened to me out of the way, I'm eager to get back to my career path. And the first step in that direction is this book. The first step is to get my message out there. The first step is to communicate some important things to the world. The first step is to communicate with you.

What comes after that? Well, I can pick up where I left off. There's nothing to stop me from going back to the University of Washington and going for my master's degree. There's nothing to stop me after that and go for that PhD and a professorship either. The sky's the limit.

It takes a couple of years to get a master's degree and a few more to get a PhD. Over the course of the last seven years, by now I might have been an associate professor at some college or university somewhere. Given the way that I'm driven, that might have even been a full professorship by now. But no crying over spilled milk for me!

So alternatively, I could make use of what I've gone through these last seven years and use the university of my experience to teach what I've learned. In fact, I hope that I've already succeeded in doing that with this book. I hope I've taught you a thing or two you didn't already know. I suspect that I've raised your awareness. I hope, by communicating all this to you, that the world will be a better place, and that you'll be a more knowledgeable person.

I'm pretty sure the world needs a kick in the butt in that department. Early on in my journey, I was interviewed on a local afternoon TV show. Toward the end of the interview, a host of the program asked, "How does it feel to be disfigured?"

There is so much wrong with that. Where do I begin? For starters, there was my inside voice—which I kept to myself, of course. I really wanted to respond, "How does it feel to be an obese, insensitive, ignorant bitch?" Of course I didn't say it out loud, but I wanted to!

Instead, I felt my face with my hands and politely and humorously responded, "Feels fine to me!"

Sure, that question was insensitive, and it provoked some insensitive thoughts on my part. Why? Beyond the obvious? Beyond that, that question displayed a lot of other things that are wrong with how we treat each other, how we act, and how we think. What do you think those things might be? Well, the "professor" in me will leave that as an exercise for you to think about on your own time. Your assignment is to ponder these questions, discuss them among yourselves and try to come up with as many examples as you can think of—especially if they're things that never occurred to you before.

Why am I assigning you this little project? That's what real teachers do. They teach you to learn how to learn.

I have two closing messages, before I let you go:

The first message regards my thoughts about what we think we know and if we question that enough. A lot of assumptions were made about me and my condition, from the time of my accident and in the weeks, months, and years that followed. Decisions were made based on those assumptions, which inhibited my ability to be part of the solution. Many not-too-well-thought-out responses and attitudes impeded my recovery and, at the beginning, damn near killed me. If not for the heroic efforts of some well-trained paramedics and a neurosurgeon who carried out his duty in performing a sanity check as part of hospital procedures, my organs would be in other people's bodies, and I'd be dead.

I'm sure many people meant well and worked hard and thought they were doing the right thing; otherwise, I wouldn't be here.

I'm equally sure that there is an opportunity for improvement as well. Based on my experience, that needs to begin with acknowledging that all knowledge is imperfect and that we need to ask more questions and be prepared to listen to and actually consider the answers we receive—and we need to do that all the time.

My second message follows from the first: You think you've got problems? Obstacles in your life? Some major setback got you down? Is it true? Do you? Really?

Question that, and get ready for the answers.

If that's true, keep at it. Find a way through it all. Fight. Search. Struggle. Fail and try again and again and again.

I did. And look at me now. For now . . . I'm out!

APPENDIX

Maria before the accident

Uncle Bobby, Maria and her cousin with their Christmas jack winnings

Christmas present wrappings

Kristina, Aunt Susan and Maria

Maria and her cousin Kristina

What Maria looks like now . . . Under her skin

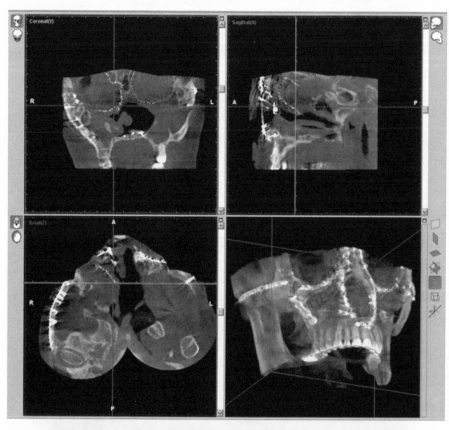

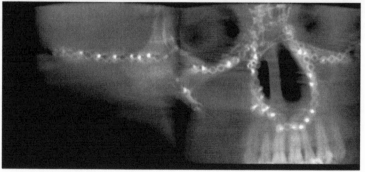

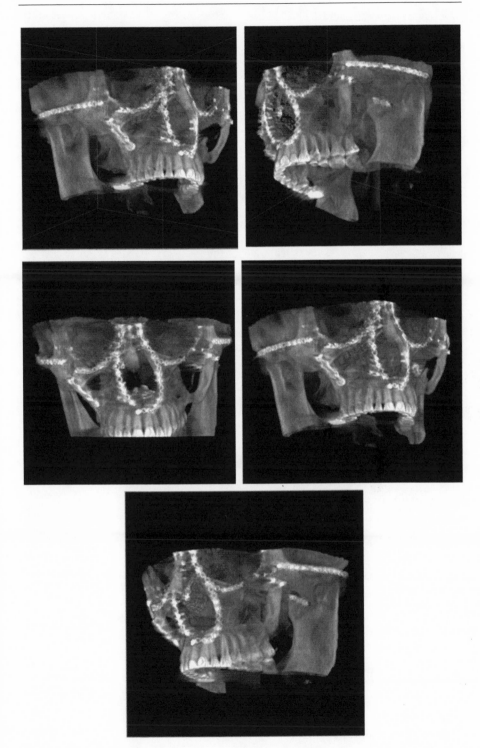

INDEX